"For years I've been saying that young believers need 'two *whys* for every *what*.' It's not enough to explain *what* the Bible says; we need to explain *why* it's true and *why* it matters. In *Why You Matter*, Mike Sherrard tackles the second *why* question with biblical accuracy and wisdom. What makes life meaningful? Why does God matter? How can we find joy in our identity? How can we love our enemies and endure hardship? If you're looking for answers to these incredibly timely questions, *Why You Matter* just may be the most important book you'll read this year."

**J. Warner Wallace**, *Dateline* featured cold-case detective, senior fellow at the Colson Center for Christian Worldview, and author of *Cold-Case Christianity* and *So the Next Generation Will Know*

"Does my life really have any meaning? If so, how do I find it? Even though our lives are busy, we all think about these questions. I am grateful that my friend Mike Sherrard has tackled these vital questions in *Why You Matter*. He pushes back against many of the cultural narratives today and looks to Jesus, and the biblical worldview, to find the ultimate answer. It shouldn't surprise you, but his answer is *yes*. Whether Christian or not, read this book and find out why your life matters deeply."

**Sean McDowell**, PhD, associate professor of apologetics at Biola University and author or coauthor of over eighteen books, including *Evidence That Demands a Verdict*

"Dignity. Equality. Human value. We take these ideas for granted but find ourselves in a vast and dangerous experiment: Can we sustain these cultural goods while we, at the same time, reject their only Source? All around us, individuals are being sacrificed to various collective agendas not delivering what they promise. In this very important book, Mike deals with humanity's most basic question, reveals why its pursuit seems so elusive to so many, and points to the only One who can offer an answer worth believing."

**John Stonestreet**, president at the Colson Center
for Christian Worldview and coauthor
of *A Practical Guide to Culture*

"As our culture becomes increasingly secular, more and more people are searching for meaning in all the wrong places—often with tragic outcomes for both mental and physical health. Mike beautifully explains why a search for meaning in the absence of God is meaningless itself, and why it's only by finding our meaning *in* God that we will experience true and lasting joy. His thoughtful and compassionate approach makes this one of those rare books that's perfect to give both your Christian and non-Christian friends! Highly recommended."

**Natasha Crain**, speaker, blogger, and author of three
books including *Talking with Your Kids about Jesus*

"Is there life that is unworthy of life? In this book, Mike Sherrard invites us to think deeply about one of life's most fundamental and significant questions: Why does life matter? Throughout this book, he demonstrates that the only rationally and psychologically compelling answer is grounded in God. But this is not merely an academic exercise. Mike's pastoral heart bursts through as he shows how our intrinsic value as God's image bearers spills over into every area of life. Identity. Love. Work. Racial justice. Sexuality. Struggles. No aspect of life is left untouched. In the end you will be able to declare with conviction, all lives matter and all of our life matters."

"Michael Sherrard engages the most pressing question of our day: Why do humans matter in the first place? That single question impacts everything from public policy to how we prepare for eternity. With so much at stake, it's tragic so few of us take time to seriously ponder it. And that's precisely what Sherrard invites us to do. Instead of plucking answers out of thin air, we need a plausible foundation for human dignity and human equality. Mike points us to the only one that works. His book is clear, thoughtful, and carefully argued. And it's accessible. I've known Mike for years, both as a dear friend and a valued coapologist. This man truly lives out what he teaches. I'm overjoyed to enthusiastically commend his latest work to you!"

"If you have ever struggled with depression, despair, and confusion, if you've ever questioned whether your life matters—or whether anything matters at all—this book is for you. From the crucible of personal experience, Michael Sherrard tells us how he and his family have dealt with soul-searing pain and how the presence of God provides hope and meaning in the face of the realities of living in a fallen world. Here is truth, hope, meaning, and a reminder of why it all matters."

C. Ben Mitchell, PhD, Graves Professor of Moral
Philosophy, Union University

"Meaning is meant. It is intended and given by a mind. If there is a meaning to all of life, one that transcends my subjective desires or thoughts, then it can only be because a Mind gave it meaning. Everyone, from an atheist to a Christian, seeks happiness and meaning in life. And many find themselves failing to live the good life. This book suggests why you may not be experiencing a meaningful life and how you can experience joy even amid hardship. The author, transparent with his own life, walks us through how he's found meaning through the good and the bad and shares how this is available—within our grasp—for everyone."

**Corey Miller,** PhD, president of Ratio Christi and author
of *In Search of the Good Life: Through the Eyes
of Aristotle, Maimonides, and Aquinas* and *Engaging
with Mormons: Understanding Their World;
Sharing Good News*

WHY
YOU
MATTER

Perspectives: A Summit Ministries Series

# WHY YOU MATTER

## MATTER

How Your Quest for Meaning
Is Meaningless without God

# MICHAEL SHERRARD

BakerBooks

a division of Baker Publishing Group
Grand Rapids, Michigan

© 2021 by Michael Sherrard

Published by Baker Books
a division of Baker Publishing Group
PO Box 6287, Grand Rapids, MI 49516-6287
www.bakerbooks.com

Library of Congress Cataloging-in-Publication Data
Names: Sherrard, Michael C., 1979– author.
Title: Why you matter : how your quest for meaning is meaningless without God / Michael Sherrard.
Description: Grand Rapids, Michigan : Baker Books, a division of Baker Publishing Group, [2021] | Series: Perspectives
Identifiers: LCCN 2020042364 | ISBN 9781540900364 (paperback) | ISBN 9781540901569 (casebound)
Subjects: LCSH: Life—Religious aspects—Christianity. | Meaning (Philosophy)—Religious aspects—Christianity. | God (Christianity) | Apologetics.
Classification: LCC BV4509.5 .S465 2021 | DDC 248.4—dc23
LC record available at https://lccn.loc.gov/2020042364

Scripture quotations are from The Holy Bible, English Standard Version® (ESV®), copyright © 2001 by Crossway, a publishing ministry of Good News Publishers. Used by permission. All rights reserved. ESV Text Edition: 2016

Published in association with The Bindery Agency, www.TheBindery Agency.com.

21  22  23  24  25  26  27      7  6  5  4  3  2  1

From me and my wife to our kids
and all who watch how we live,
may you never forget that nothing compares
to the greatness of knowing Jesus Christ our Lord.

# Contents

# Foreword

Regardless of what you believe, there's a good chance you are living as if atheists are right when they claim the material world is all there is. But if matter is all that matters, then you don't matter and neither do I. A purposeful life is hopelessly out of reach if chemical reactions and genetic replication are all that is real.

As the president of Summit Ministries, I work with thousands of students every year, along with their parents, grandparents, teachers, and pastors. Every one of them faces the question of identity: Who am I? What am I supposed to do? The good news is that God *exists*, and *you matter*. That's Mike Sherrard's message in the wonderful little volume you hold in your hands.

In the battle of ideas about what makes life meaningful, Mike is the kind of guy you want in the foxhole with you. I trust Mike because he believes firmly in God's truth but never sacrifices relationships in his pursuit of it. *Why You Matter* is straightforward and utterly transparent, sometimes alarmingly so. It's the kind of book that can only be written by someone who has been there, someone whose faith is growing *because* of life's difficulties and not despite them.

"The pursuit of a meaningful life is about both knowing and feeling that our life matters," Mike says. "Each of us is driven to find the peace and joy, a sense of rest and fulfillment—that feeling of being home—that comes from knowing that our actions and lives really matter, that we truly have a meaningful life."

In *Why You Matter*, Mike shows how your life has meaning, where that meaning comes from, and how to live meaningfully, even joyfully. In the waiting. In hardship. In worrisome times. This book isn't long, but it is challenging. Think of Mike as a friendly guide through the unpredictable wilderness of modern life to the glorious summit of God's truth. Like all wilderness guides, Mike constantly encourages you, but he also pushes you to grow in a way that makes that encouragement meaningful.

I can't think of a more important topic right now than identity, or more important truths than that God exists—and you matter.

Jeff Myers, PhD, president of Summit Ministries,
Manitou Springs, Colorado, September 2020

# Acknowledgments

Thank you to Jeff Myers, Aaron Klemm, Jason Graham, and those at Summit Ministries for the great work you do, the thousands of young lives you have changed, and for making this book project a reality.

Thank you to my dear friend and mentor Scott Klusendorf. There is no doubt in my mind: I would never have been afforded the chance to write this book without everything you have done for me. Your friendship and wisdom have made more of a difference in my and my family's life than you will ever realize. And that's good. The world would not be able to handle your pride.

Thank you to my friend Barbara Toth, who read every word in this book and helped me cross the finish line. The words herein bear your insight and prayers.

And to my wife, thank you for your perseverance and love. Our life is not an easy one, but the Lord has held us close so far. He will for many more years. Thank you for being tough and sweet, one I can trust, and one I can love.

# Prologue

## *Why I Couldn't Write This Book*

The last several years have been hard on me and my family. We have known death, sickness, sadness, anxiety, disability, loneliness, and betrayal. And betrayal is worse than all the others. It is like a living death. Yet through the pain, one of the things that has kept me steady is the knowledge of what makes life meaningful. It has been an anchor for me and my family. It anchors me when I think about the uncertain future of my oldest son, who has the rarest of rare genetic disorders. It anchors me when I face the reality that all I'm good at might be taken away. It anchors me when my wife and I fight. And it anchors me when I worry that others might not think that my life matters.

The knowledge of why I matter has saved me and my family. It has given us joy and the strength to persevere in hard times. I want to pass on what I know. It's relevant for all of us, old and young. For the old, this knowledge can restore what is broken, renew what is getting rusty, and redeem the rest of life. For the young, this knowledge can free them to live securely in who they are, help them resist many of life's temptations, and keep them from experiencing unnecessary pain. Why we matter is something we all struggle with, and in this common struggle there is something strangely encouraging: we are in this together.

Knowing why we matter is important for all of us, but it is especially important for the young. I know I am old for many reasons. I tell stories every ten minutes, I have thrown out my back by sneezing, and I know things I wish I would have known twenty years ago. Every old man says, "If I could have known this at your age . . ." Well, as patronizing as it might sound, this book contains a ton of stuff I wish my twenty-year-old self could have read. And since it is usually better to avoid making mistakes than to have to redeem them, I embrace this old-man quality and will share what I have learned with whoever is willing to listen.

It has to be difficult growing up today. Everyone has an agenda, or so it seems, and with social media everyone has a platform. Every day, we are confronted with ideas and arguments seeking our allegiance. But what is real? Who should we trust? Who should we follow? Who has the words of life? Well, it's not me. It's Jesus. In him alone is true life. And I want to be able to show you what life in him looks like. I want you to start your life off in the right direction or get back on track if you're lost. I want to be able to write this book.

As I write this prologue, it's April 17, 2020, and I'm only about a month away from my manuscript deadline, but I have nothing. Not literally nothing—I have thousands of words that I hate. It's something I'd be fine handing in to a professor who would half-read it and give me a fair grade, but it's not something I'd like to give a friend to read at night unless they've already had a glass of wine or two.

I just can't get into the flow, that creative space where time vanishes and I am discovering what I'm creating. For the longest time it has felt like I haven't had permission to write this book. I won't go much into what that means, mostly because I'm not sure I understand it completely. It just seems to be the right way to describe what I'm experiencing. Whenever I carve out time to write (or my wife graciously gives me some), nothing good comes of it. I feel like I am betraying my family and my church, that there is something else I am supposed to be doing. I'm a pastor, and the needs of even a small church weigh heavily. There is always a marriage hurting, somebody battling depression, a relationship problem, and, well, you've likely been to church before—you know.

Interestingly, though, throughout the pressures of meeting a deadline, contemplating the humiliation of not delivering, and battling the hardships we have faced over the last several years, the one thing I haven't struggled with is my worth or my identity. My challenges haven't caused me to question whether my life matters or not. I think I have already learned the lessons needed to persevere in hard times, which is why I think the Lord has given me the opportunity to write this book.

If you are reading this, I suppose I found my permission. Or I just crossed my fingers, turned in the assignment, and sent my editor a bottle of his favorite whiskey.

Now it's September, and the whole world is still in the midst of the COVID-19 pandemic and America is suffering the pain of racial injustice. 2020 has been quite a year. I am not sure what, if anything, that means for this book. *Why You Matter* is scheduled to be released in the spring of 2021, when the world will be either in way worse shape or putting itself back together. I'm wondering if this crisis has many of us rethinking what matters in life, and why our lives matter in the first place. I have heard many people use the term *reset* in trying to find some good in all the trials this year has brought us. And a reset is a nice idea. It isn't often that we get the chance to reset things. Maybe this is the gift the Lord has given us in this season. I hope it is the kind of gift I can give you in this book: a reset of what you think about yourself, your significance, your purpose, and your value— why you matter.

# Introduction

## *It's Time to Figure Out Why You Matter*

It is a confusing time to be alive. "All lives matter" is an offensive phrase, Aunt Jemimah is a symbol of white supremacy, and going to church might get you arrested, but burning down a city won't. What in the world is going on?

In a very objective sense, the United States is the freest, most prosperous, and most equitable country in the history of humankind. Cognitive psychologist Steven Pinker details in his data-driven book *Enlightenment Now* (which Bill Gates says is his new favorite book, for whatever that's worth) how the world, not just America, is in a far better place than it has ever been, according to every metric available. Pinker said that those who try to offer a doom-and-gloom assessment of the state of the world are wrong. "And not just a little wrong—wrong, wrong, flat-earth wrong, couldn't-*be*-more-wrong."[1] I wonder what Steven really thinks.

To Pinker's point, during the previous decade, we saw record employment for minorities,[2] the continuing downward trend of violent crimes,[3] the legalization of gay marriage, the continued expansion of LGBT rights,[4] and the second term of our country's first black president. And regardless of what you think about capitalism, the current state of the police, the success of Obama's presidency, or the morality of LGBTQ-related issues, it is clear that many have been working hard to see that all people can live out the foundational beliefs that formed America. All people are endowed by their Creator with certain inalienable rights and should be free to pursue a life of happiness. And for the last 250 years, Americans have been destroying one form of oppression after another, seeking to right wrongs and create a free and fair world for all.

Then came 2020, and many would have us believe that Americans have been working to create a caste system of oppression for the last 250 years without fail. So which is it? Is this country the freest, most prosperous, and most equitable country in the history of the world, or a land of greedy racist oppressors?

Well, it's kind of both. This shouldn't surprise us. Life is more complicated and nuanced than political slogans and social media sound bites. There is almost always another side to the story if we are willing to hear it.

Racism—both institutional and relational (i.e., hate crimes)—is illegal, and there are still racists.[5] Freedom and democratic governments like ours are spreading across the globe,[6] and so is human trafficking.[7] Capitalism is taking the world, not just the United States, out of extreme poverty and into a quality of life never seen before in the history of humankind.[8] Yet the financial fruits of this growth seem much slower in coming to those who are struggling the most.[9]

All lives certainly do matter—it's what our pursuit of equality is all about—and that is most assuredly an offensive phrase when used in a dismissive manner in response to a social justice movement.[10] Mass gatherings should take into account the health risk to others in the midst of a pandemic, but church services ought not be singled out. Aunt Jemimah—yeah, I'm not so sure about this one. A symbol of oppression? That seems a bit obnoxious. I do know that people are not justified in burning down a city to make a political statement, though we do need to take into consideration what drove these masses to such violent ends.

Again, it is a confusing time to be alive.

America is the land of the free, the prosperous, the hurting, and the broken all at the same time. Much good work has been done, and more is needed. But there is hope. Underneath all of the confusion, fighting, and ideological polarization, there is, strangely enough, some unity. It seems there are more people than not who are committed to the idea that all people should be treated with equal dignity and respect.

Ask your neighbor, your son or daughter, or your coworker if they think all people should be treated equally. I bet you could ask all the people you know and not find one person advocating for the oppression of any people group. Now, you will certainly find differences in how to achieve equality and what it looks like. Some will disagree, for example, on whether equality of opportunity or equality of outcome is the goal. But that is a very different conversation, and you would be talking to a very different kind of person than the one who thinks some people are subhuman and should be treated accordingly.

There is hope for a people who all generally agree we should not be free to unjustly discriminate against anyone based on some arbitrary characteristic.

But why do so many people believe in equality? Though it may seem common sense today to believe that all people matter and should be treated equally, historically this has been an elusive idea. History is filled with examples of how one group of people dehumanized another. Plato and Aristotle argued that women were inferior to men.[11] Aquinas seemed to have considered the image of God as amounting to nothing in the mentally compromised.[12] We, of course, know about the Nazis, but few realize that there was a eugenics movement spreading across the United States at the same time.[13] And concerning the country built on inalienable rights, maybe your grandfather could tell a story of not being allowed to drink at a certain water fountain, sit where he liked on a bus, or eat where he pleased.

Some of the best thinkers and leaders in history believed in or tolerated discrimination on the basis of things like color, gender, and cognitive ability. Why was this unjust discrimination so common in history? Racism, for example, is such a ridiculous idea, right? Skin color has no bearing on human value and significance. Neither does gender, cognitive ability, or anything else. Possessing or not possessing certain arbitrary characteristics is no basis for determining human value and significance. Agree? I'm quite sure you do. So how did anyone come to believe otherwise and act according to the conviction that human value comes in degrees based on certain arbitrary characteristics? Thank goodness we've become more enlightened and have jettisoned these barbaric beliefs.

But do we know why we believe in equality?

## A Time for Reflection, Not Just Action

If we're really pressed, don't we still think that some lives are more valuable than others? Aren't there some people whom the world would be better off without? What are our real thoughts about Democrats or those involved in the pro-life movement? Don't we think we're better than those people? Okay, maybe we don't believe that, but I'm quite sure we've all had these kinds of thoughts before. Why did we reject them? Why didn't we act on our hateful inclinations?

Maybe it was simply because we were cowards and feared legal repercussions. Perhaps in another time and another place we would have found our knee on someone's neck or found ourselves lighting the match that burned down our city because we knew we could get away with it. Or maybe we aren't cowards, and it was the grace of God that kept us from becoming monsters. Nearly all who do the unthinkable once thought it impossible for them as well. Six-year-olds dream of saving the world, not watching it burn.

Maybe it wasn't just luck or providence. Perhaps it was the belief that all lives matter and should be treated with equal dignity and respect. I do think that belief has stopped many in their hateful tracks. But why is that a true belief? I'm glad we have it, but what is our justification for believing it? If we cannot answer why all people are equal, there is a very good chance we will apply this belief inconsistently based on self-interest or be persuaded to leave it behind by a clever professor or a power-hungry mob.

So what is it about human life that convinces you that all lives matter regardless of race, gender, class, accomplishment, characteristic, or anything else? Do they? Do all lives really matter? Does yours? And if so, why does it matter? What makes your life just as meaningful and significant as everyone else's? Your answer must be good enough to support your conviction. Is it?

Let's do a thought experiment and maybe shed some light on your assumptions regarding human value and equality. Suppose you could drastically improve the lives of countless people both now and in the future by killing a million innocent children each year. Should you kill them? What if it was the only means to save our way of life? What if all the children were unwanted? What if they were suffering? What if they were cognitively disabled? What if they were just moments after birth, or moments before? Would you kill them then?[14]

Maybe you have an answer, and maybe you came to it quickly. Maybe you had to think about it, or maybe it changed as you read on. I am actually not concerned with your answer. I'm concerned with your reasoning. The really important question isn't what you would do but why you would do it. On what basis did you decide to kill or not kill the innocent children? How do you decide what makes a human life valuable and worth protecting?

Wrapped up in the issue of equality are our assumptions about what makes life valuable and worth living—why we matter. But why we all matter equally is not a belief that can survive assumptions. We need to know why all lives matter, including our own, and our answer can't be, "Well, they just do."

So, again, what is your justification for your belief that all lives matter? How do you defend equality? And how do you know that your own life is worth anything? I think you'll come to find out that these questions aren't so easy to answer, and you might not actually possess the sort of convictions that lead to equality or the ability to truly believe that your life matters.

## A Crisis of Meaning

When it comes to equality, we are all seemingly living in the state of "I believe. Help me in my unbelief."[15] We believe all lives matter the same, but we don't know why it's a true belief, and therefore we don't know how to apply it consistently. When we don't know the reason someone should be treated with dignity and respect, it makes it easy to hate them.

For example, how would you describe the state of public discourse these days? Informed, respectful, and productive? Of course not. More times than I can remember, people today hate those who disagree with them and seek to shut up opponents by any means rather than argue reasonably.[16] Western civilization, America at least, isn't an example of civility, is it? One would think that a people who believed in equality would have actions consistent with that belief and be able to be civil and show respect to people with whom there is disagreement. Not so with us. It's like we are all charging into battle screaming "Die!" in the name of equality.

Ironically, our quest for equality is marked by things like political and conversational strategies that rely on the degradation of one's opponents. If we find someone who doesn't agree with us, it is because they are vile scum—evil, murderous, bigoted, loathsome human beings whom the world would be better off without, or so we're told. Tolerance is officially dead. Its blood is drying on the hands of the cancel-culture mob. It is now agree or else. The things that are done in the name of equality are astounding.

Moreover, if we truly understood why all lives matter, including our own, why are psychological illnesses like anxiety disorders and depression skyrocketing?[17] Why are teenage suicide rates increasing?[18] Why are more people feeling lonely when we are more connected than ever through technology?[19] What are we missing? It seems as though we believe that all lives *can* matter, not that all lives *do* matter. And that is a big difference.

We are in a crisis of meaning. It seems we have lost the knowledge of what makes our lives meaningful. We have forgotten why we are valuable, all valuable, and equally so. It's why we hate. It's why we fight. It's why we struggle with self-worth. It's why it's getting harder to get out of bed. It will be our undoing as a nation and a burden that we will only be able to carry for so long. We really need to know why we matter.

## A Battle of Ideas

This crisis of meaning is one of the casualties of the growing secularism in our country. When you take Western civilization off of its Christian moorings, one of the things you lose is the anchor of life's meaning and human value.

We are immersed in a battle of ideas about what makes life meaningful. On one side, you have the remnants of the Christian worldview that believe life is inherently meaningful because it is the handiwork of God, and humans are intrinsically valuable because we are made in his image. On the other side, you have the worldviews that deny God's existence and argue that life is inherently meaningless because it is the work of random chemical reactions and genetic mutations, but meaning and value can be created by us through our choices.

This is a big difference with profound consequences. It is the difference between living out a life of meaning and constructing one out of nothing. Throughout this book, I hope to show clearly what is at stake for our quest for meaning if God does not exist. I also hope to show how much we've been influenced by a worldview we reject. Both Christians and atheists tend not to realize how much they borrow from each other's worldviews.

As you begin to consider what makes life meaningful and why we all matter, step one is to consider if you are coasting on borrowed assumptions rather than being driven by sound and coherent beliefs. In this crisis of meaning, you might be surprised to learn how many contradictory beliefs and assumptions are in your head right now. One way to find out is to question your beliefs.

Why does your life matter? Why is it worth the same as everyone else's? What do you feel about your own life? Do you feel like something is missing? Do you feel fulfilled? Why or why not? What is your sense of self-worth based on? Is it your relationships, your bank account, your accomplishments? What gives you the assurance that your life is meaningful? What if those things were taken away? Would you still feel the same about yourself?

So how did you answer these questions? You probably should write your answers down. Seriously, write down what you think makes life meaningful and why we all matter. Then ask yourself if these beliefs came from Christianity or something else.

Seeing your own beliefs on paper is a powerful experience. Often it makes you say, "I believe that?" Reflecting on and writing down your beliefs may be the most illuminating things you get from this book. Your answers to the above questions are part of your foundation. Let's make sure you know what you've built your life on.

## A Reason to Be Hopeful

Though this is a tough time, there is a reason to be hopeful. We are not the first people to experience turmoil, and you are not the first person to question the significance of your life. I think why we matter is the issue of our time, and I believe understanding it will bring us and our country peace.

Based on the title of this book, you know where I'm coming from. I am a Christian. I make no apologies about that. I believe that God exists and that he has revealed himself to his creation. I believe life is inherently meaningful because it is the work of God. I believe we are made in his image and are thus instilled with unimaginable dignity, worth, and purpose. This belief is the justification for my belief in equality, and it provides clarity on so many other important issues of our time. It is what will lead us to discover lives of meaning and joy like nothing else can.

I believe I have good reasons for my beliefs. I hope to persuade you that they are true and that your quest for meaning is meaningless without God.

God does exist, and you matter. Maybe not for the reasons

you think, but your life has significance. It has value. It has purpose. It would make a difference if you were not alive. Now, you may not feel that way at the moment, and for that, I'm sorry. This world is often a cruel place—broken, merciless, and unforgiving. Yet there is beauty, goodness, grace, and hope for you. Deep down you believe this. I believe it. Now it's time to see if we can become certain of it.

If you are questioning the relevance of your life, you are not alone. Nearly all of us do. But I want you to do something. I want you to challenge your doubts. Why should you believe them? What authority do they have? Where did they come from? What standard are you using to judge if your life matters? There is one Judge, and I can nearly guarantee that what you think has made your life insignificant is not what he thinks.

You may have heard your whole life that you are nothing. You may be struggling to let go of a really bad mistake. You may have been the victim of some evil act. You may have lost or hate your job. You may have just had your best friend betray you. But while friends, accomplishments, careers, and a lack of hardship are all good things, they are not what gets to determine the meaning of your life.

It's time to build a better foundation for your life and move off the shifting sands. It's time to embrace the reality that you matter because you are made in God's image. Can you even begin to conceive of the value and dignity of being made in the likeness of God, the being of incommensurate worth, goodness, and beauty? Understanding this changes everything. It will transform what you think about your identity, your calling, your ethics, your hardship, your apathy, and your chance for true fulfillment.

Maybe you've never heard this teaching. Maybe you have, and it's worn out on you. Or maybe you don't believe in God and this sounds like nothing more than myth. Fair enough. Challenge me throughout this book. Write objections to my arguments in the margins. I'm not offended. All I ask is that you humbly consider the fact that maybe you haven't been a good judge of your importance. If that's the case, the good news is that what awaits you is the joyful discovery of why you matter.

# What Makes
# Our Lives Meaningful?

In thinking about what gives life meaning, I'm reminded of a joke my dad told when I was growing up. And if there is one thing we know about dad jokes, it's that they are the best. Of course, I have to say this as a father of five who has already experienced many times over the joy of seeing a five-year-old give me their best teenage eye roll after one of my jokes. But it is my duty and the duty of all fathers to be lame and embarrass their children. I take this job seriously, as did my father before me.

The joke my dad told is not original to him. It's more like a story, and it goes like this. There were four people on a plane traveling to . . . well, it doesn't make a difference where they were going. What does make a difference is who the four were: a priest, a scientist, a student, and a pilot, of course. Halfway through the flight, the pilot burst into the cabin with fear in his eyes and defeat in his tone and said, "The plane is going down, we have to jump, and there are only three parachutes."

The four looked at one another, fearing to say what they were thinking. The scientist spoke first. "I'm sorry, but I'm quite too important to die. I have one of the highest IQs ever recorded. My mind is too valuable to lose. I'm sorry!" And before the other three could say a word, the scientist grabbed a pack and jumped out of the plane.

The pilot spoke next. "You two take the parachutes. I'm the captain—I'll go down with the plane."

The pilot's courage spread to the priest, who promptly said, "No, I'm old and have lived a good life. I know where I'm going when I die. You two take the parachutes. I'm content to die."

The student tried to speak, but the pilot and the priest ignored his petition as they argued about why the other ought to take the parachute. Finally, the student was able to break through. "Hey! Listen! We can all jump!"

"No. There were only three parachutes, son," the priest said.

"There are still three parachutes!" the student exclaimed. "The smartest person on the planet just jumped out of the plane with my backpack!"

What I think we all like about this joke at some level is that the scientist got the poetic justice he deserved. He believed his intellect justified his life, and it was his "intellect" that killed him. I mean, who was he to think that his life was more important than the lives of the others? Just because he scored high on a test? Smart people aren't worth more than the rest of us. Intelligence isn't what makes life meaningful. Tests do not determine significance. Or do they?

Prenatal children diagnosed with Down syndrome have little chance of escaping abortion.[1] Why is that? And do not try to say this is simply a matter of a woman's choice. It certainly is a matter of choice, but choice on the basis of a perceived disability. At such a high rate of abortion, it is undeniable that many of these fetuses would not have been aborted had they not had Down syndrome. It wasn't the pregnancy that was unwanted; it was the child with Down syndrome.

So what is believed about people with Down syndrome and their ability to have a meaningful life that would lead so many otherwise excited and expectant parents to choose abortion? Is it their facial features? Is it their health complications? Is it their different emotional or relational skills that disqualify them from possessing a meaningful life? Or maybe it's their mild, moderate, or low IQ scores? Is it because they will likely never dominate the NBA, be a senator, or invent the next must-have vain gadget? What is it?

We would never publicly say that life is only meaningful and worth living if you look a certain way, have "normal" relationships, possess a certain IQ, have no health complications, or can accomplish something the rest of us deem worthy. But maybe it's what we really believe. What else can explain why so many choose abortion after learning the results of a prenatal test? I think we are a confused people.[2] On the one hand, we reject the idea that there are some more deserving of life, dignity, and respect than others, and on the other hand, we are willing to perform mercy killings in the womb to spare some of a life deemed unworthy.

## Why You Matter, Matters

The belief about what makes life meaningful is not a belief that can afford any ambiguity. The stakes are too high. When we don't understand why we matter, we risk not just our own sense of fulfillment in life but our ability to treat each other as equals. Misunderstanding this topic is what allows us to declare some lives unworthy, even our own. So, let's get into this and see if we can sort out why we matter.

The first thing we need to realize is that we are all using some standard to judge if our life is meaningful. Whether it's our feelings or something else, there is something every one of us looks to in determining if our life is measuring up or not. This is because we all need to answer really important questions, such as, What's the point of it all? Why am I here? Would it make a difference if I didn't exist? What is the reason I should get out of bed?

Some of you have no answer for that last question. Each morning is a struggle to shed your covers, and each night is a fight to allow another morning to come. Sadness is seemingly your only companion, and you are seriously entertaining saying goodbye to him too. But though you may feel as though your life has no reason to continue, it objectively does. Your life's meaning is not equal to your happiness. Your feelings are not the judge of your life's worth.[3]

Happiness is a fickle master and a terrible judge of a meaningful life. Even bad things can make us happy. We all have done things that at the time made us feel good, but upon growth and reflection, we realized how awful our deeds were. If happiness is the measure of meaning, then the scales will never be still. But even if our happiness is unwavering and doesn't come at the expense of another, it is hard to imagine calling a life meaningful simply because it is a happy life. Drugs are euphoric, and if that is all there is to life's meaning, then give us some pills, turn off the lights, and let us dream as many happy dreams as we can.

Of course happiness is good, and praise the Lord for the times in which we are truly happy. But I think we all would agree that life can be meaningful and sad, which, ironically, is a kind of happy news. No, more than happy. I think you and I would agree that when we talk about a meaningful life, we are talking about something deeper than happiness. We are talking about a purpose that leads to joy, something powerful enough to sustain us even when laughter has abandoned us.

So if it's not simply happiness, what determines if our lives are meaningful? Or, I suppose I should say, who determines if our lives are meaningful—us or God? These are the two options in the quest for meaning, and they are drastically different. The one thing they have in common is the need for a creator. Meaning doesn't come from nothing.

## Who Creates Your Life's Meaning? You or God?

Christianity claims that life is inherently meaningful because it is the handiwork of God. Life was made on purpose for a purpose, and thus all of life has an objective reason for its existence whether we feel like it does or not. Christianity also claims that our lives are intrinsically valuable because we are loved by God and made in his image. We are valuable by virtue of what we are, not what we can do or become. Our value is a permanent part of our nature. It does not need to be acquired; it's intrinsic.

Life's inherent meaning and intrinsic human value are pillars for the Christian belief in a meaningful life. Value that is rooted in our nature as opposed to some characteristic we might or might not have gives rise to equality. Because we each equally share the same value-giving property—our nature—all people are equally valuable. Therefore, all people should be treated with equal dignity and respect and be afforded equal opportunity to live out their valuable lives within the purposeful boundaries of their Creator's design.

And God's design is truly remarkable. According to Christianity, what we are made for is far more amazing than we realize. The trite answer "to glorify God" that may have been drilled into us by a Sunday school teacher is not a wrong answer, but what it means to glorify God is something far richer than simply abstaining from this, saying no to that, and singing pathetically cheap and repetitious love songs packaged as worship music. Before we cast aside the dignity of glorifying God, we really should understand what it means.

But that's all I can say about that for now. A fuller understanding of your purpose and value and how it can lead to fulfillment will have to wait another chapter or so. For now, it is sufficient to know that the Christian claim is that your life is imbued with both meaning and value from the start, apart from your actions. Your life, in other words, is already and has always been unimaginably valuable and filled with objective meaning. The exact opposite is true if there is no Creator.

If God does not exist, then life has no inherent meaning, and human life is not intrinsically valuable. This is not to say that those who do not believe in God live sad, unfulfilled lives without any purpose. Quite the contrary. Many atheists believe their life is meaningful and satisfying as much as those who believe in God. They have convictions and values that they are quite passionate about. This is not in dispute, and it is not my claim. I would argue that many atheists live good lives. Many are nicer, happier, more charitable, and better thinkers than many Christians I've known. Rather, my claim, and one that is commonly held by atheists, is that if God does not exist, then life began as a blank slate without any meaning or value.

First, meaning cannot be an inherent part of the nature of an accidental universe. Without a Creator, the universe and all of life in it exist for no reason at all. Life is merely the result of a cosmic accident: unguided chemical reactions and random genetic mutations. There is no reason something rather than nothing exists. Life just happened to happen.

Even if some would argue that the evolution of life was guided in a sense by the laws of physics and natural selection, unless physics and natural selection are the product of a mind, they are just as arbitrary as anything else. Whatever "guide" might mean, it cannot mean direction toward an end goal. A goal is the product of a mind. With no mind, there can be no goal, no grand purpose for it all. Things are the way they are just because they are. If life is the result of this random and arbitrary process, it cannot possess meaning as an essential component of its nature. It's inherently meaningless. Life is what it is just because it is. As Richard Dawkins famously put it,

> In a universe of blind physical forces and genetic replication, some people are going to get hurt, other people are going to get lucky, and you won't find any rhyme or reason in it, nor any justice. The universe we observe has precisely the properties we should expect if there is, at bottom, *no design, no purpose, no evil and no good, nothing but blind, pitiless indifference.* . . . DNA neither knows nor cares. DNA just is. And we dance to its music.[4]

Second, if human life is the result of this random process, it wouldn't be valuable in and of itself. Something has intrinsic value if it is an end in itself rather than a means to some end. If human life was not designed and made for a purpose, it cannot be an end. At best, human life can be a means to an end, and its value would therefore be extrinsic, like money. Money has no value in and of itself. It is just paper, coin, or code. Money has value because it's a useful means to an end. It's functionally valuable.

If human life is the product of evolution, it is just flesh and bones. It isn't valuable in and of itself any more than, say, a cockroach. Human life might become more valuable than a cockroach if it possesses certain characteristics that are found to be a useful means toward some preferable end, but it does not start out more valuable. As bioethicist Peter Singer once put it, "The notion that human life is sacred just because it is human life is medieval."[5] In an accidental universe, humans are not valuable because of what they are but because of what they can do.[6]

According to many atheists, the fact that human life is inherently meaningless and begins without value doesn't mean that we have to become nihilists who believe nothing matters. Meaning can be created by us. And though human nature isn't intrinsically valuable, many argue that personhood is functionally valuable and can serve as the basis for equality. We will explore these claims in the next chapter and see if they hold up. Before that, we need to consider something else.

## What Is Your Starting Point?

If God exists, meaning is inherent to life, and human value is fixed and rooted in the kind of thing it is: a human life. If God does not exist, life is inherently meaningless and worthless, though it might become valuable by virtue of what it can do or become. We either steward a meaningful life or create it. These starting points are as far from each other as the east is from the west. Consider how different they really are:

Either we are already unimaginably valuable as something made by God and loved by him, or we possess a nature with no ultimate significance or value beyond what we can create for ourselves.

Either there is an objective purpose to life that we need to discover and live out, or there is no purpose, and we have to make one up.

Either we as human beings are equally valuable because we equally share the same value-giving property— our nature made in God's image—or we might

become equally valuable if we equally obtain something that we decide makes human life valuable.

It is hard to overstate the profound difference between
a world of inherent meaning and intrinsic value and one
without them. Sometimes we are lured into thinking that
the existence of God doesn't make much of a difference in
everyday life. But as you can see, whether or not God exists
affects everything.

I wonder which is your starting point. I do hope to show
you that a meaningful life is not a destination that can be
reached from the godless starting point. However, before
looking at which position is more reasonable to believe
in, you need to ask yourself if you really believe what you
thought you did. Are you really starting your quest from
where you thought? You may have embraced components
of a reality you deny exists.

If you are a Christian, do you really believe that your life
is intrinsically valuable? Do you really believe that life has
a grand purpose in which you can live out your inherently
meaningful life? Or have you been operating out of the assumption that you must make your life worth something?

Maybe that's why you work so many hours. Maybe that's
why you jump from one relationship to the next. Maybe
that's why you're struggling with your self-worth. You may
have left the reality in which your significance comes from
being made in God's image and started living as though your
significance comes from your salary, your friends, or your
accomplishments.

If you are an atheist, do you really believe that life has no
meaning beyond what we create? Do you believe that right

and wrong are simply our creations? Do you really believe that all created meanings are equal? Or have you been operating out of the assumption that there is something of transcendent worth and meaning awaiting you to discover it, something that can anchor your convictions about life's purpose?

Maybe that's why you are so passionate about human rights and justice. Maybe that's why you sleep well when you've served someone in need. Maybe that's why you feel guilty when you've benefited at another's expense. You may have left the reality in which morality and purpose are random evolutionary constructs that allowed for our survival and started living as though there was really a divine purpose for how we should love one another as we love ourselves.

Maybe you don't really believe what you thought you did.

## Could You Change Your Mind?

Reflecting on simple things often leads to profound insights. This topic can be a confusing one, but the core of it is really quite simple. Either it is true that you live in a reality where the One who made everything knows every bit of you, loves you, and will guide you in living out a life of inherent meaning and intrinsic value, or it is true that you live in a reality where meaning and value are constructs of an evolutionary process lacking no greater significance than what you assign to them.

This is no argument. It is only an observation. But I wonder what you really think is true. Though the starting points in the quest for meaning are quite different, your starting point doesn't necessarily reflect whether you are a Christian or an atheist. Like I said before, you may profess to be one thing but live as another. The further we go along, the more you may find that though you call yourself one thing, you really believe something else.

Therefore, I want to challenge you from the outset to critically examine your beliefs with particular attention to your inconsistency. There are seemingly few who live a consistent life and hold coherent beliefs. Many of us, Christian or not, have conclusions that do not logically follow from our underlying beliefs, and we should all be eager to have those inconsistencies exposed. A life of blind faith is rather pathetic. So be brave and follow the truth wherever it takes you, and may it set you free.

This is hard. We all like to think we are open-minded and will be easily persuaded if something is true. But we won't. Very few people like being wrong, especially about beliefs upon which their life is based. So rather than entertain the idea that a belief should be changed, we'll change the subject, create straw men, inflict ad hominem attacks, and keep our minds closed. And we'll probably get angry at the one challenging our beliefs.

As William Rusher put it in his classic book *How to Win Arguments More Often Than Not*, "If someone makes us feel that we are thinking, we love him; but if he really makes us think, we hate him. . . . Nobody, confronted with a really devastating argument against something in which he has hitherto deeply believed, slaps himself on the thigh and shouts, 'By gosh, I never thought of that!'"[7]

It can be a scary notion to consider that a deeply held belief might be wrong. And I get it. I have lived my entire life according to the belief that God exists. I've led and taught other people to do the same. If God does not exist, I am to be pitied. Both Christians and atheists alike have something to lose if they are wrong. And the fear of losing something we love can cause us to cover our ears and shout rather than really listen and consider that we might be wrong.

However, there are some issues that must be considered regardless of the fear of what the changed belief might bring. This is one such topic. So be aware that anger and fear might find you as you consider what really makes your life meaningful. I rather hope this book is nothing but a joyful and fun experience. But should anger or fear visit you, know that it's fine. It is to be expected. But do not let these emotions keep you from embracing what is real.

More than just helping you find the fulfillment that comes from knowing what makes life meaningful, I hope this book causes you to consider what is really real and embrace the One who made it so. The universal quest for a meaningful life is a reason to consider the reality of God's existence. The fact that we all have the drive and desire to have a life of meaning says something about what it means to be human. Is that drive a result of evolution, or is it something else?[8] I think it is something else. Are you open to the possibility? Well, let's first see if atheism can justify the belief in a meaningful life.[9]

# Can We Make Our
# Own Lives Meaningful?

Tragedy makes us realize how much of our lives we have been wasting. It puts things into perspective, doesn't it? Those of us who have lost a loved one, gotten really sick, or even had a dear friend move away know how these experiences awaken us to what really matters. And it's not just that we realize we spend so much time on insignificant things; we tend to recognize that we shouldn't have cared about them so much in the first place.

How important is your successful career if you don't see your kids grow up? What good is your fame if you hate what you have become? And how valuable was all your athletic achievement? Was the endless practice and making the team at all costs worth it? The state championship only takes you so far. Eventually life goes on. You can only live in the glory days of high school for so long before you become that creepy old man who still wears his letterman jacket and class ring.

The examples go on and on. We've all seen a movie with this kind of script. We know we're prone to exchange the important for the trivial, yet we do it anyway. We're strange creatures who seemingly need tragedy to remind us of what really matters. And if this is so, we ought not waste the year written and produced by Stephen King. The horrible events of 2020 may lead us all to what we have been looking for.

But why are we searching for something? Why are we plagued with regret? Who cares if our lives don't measure up? Wouldn't it be freeing to know there is no standard by which we can be judged?

## Living in the Tension of a Godless Universe

After one of my lectures on the absurdity of life without God, I met a college-age girl who was quite smart, very respectful, and not easily offended. She could hold her own intellectually, and our conversation was one of the more insightful ones I've had after a lecture. She was an atheist and asked really good questions, and after several minutes, she told me a captivating story of her own struggle with the pursuit of a meaningful life.

On the one hand, she had embraced the idea for a long time that because God doesn't exist, life has no inherent meaning. This idea was liberating to her. "Life is so stressful," she told me. "As soon as you can talk, people are asking you what you want to be when you grow up, and they never stop asking that question. The pressure only grows from there: be sure to get good grades in school, try this sport, join that club, protest this, support that, pick a side, what's your backup college? It doesn't end. The idea that nothing matters in an ultimate sense is freeing.

"You see, if life has no purpose, all choices are meaningful if they matter to us. Just don't hurt anyone, and live a simple life if you want. Solve a crisis, make millions, or bake cookies your whole life—they all matter the same. You cannot fail in a universe of no purpose. That's a relief."

A good insight, isn't it? But it wasn't her whole story.

"On the other hand," she said, "it would be kind of nice to know that there was actually a real purpose to life. It would be nice to know that what I do matters in a way that's more important than just making me feel good. I get that you cannot fail if life has no ultimate purpose, but you also can't succeed. It's kind of depressing to know that all I will ever achieve are the goals I create for myself. That seems kind of pointless."[1]

What a beautiful way to describe the tension of a universe without God: living in the freedom and futility of having no objective standard to judge your actions. But was she missing something? Is there something more to the atheistic case for a meaningful life that could have resolved her problem?

## How Does Atheism Justify Belief in a Meaningful Life?

Famed atheist Richard Dawkins once asked brilliantly funny comedian and atheist Ricky Gervais why he gets up in the morning. "I think you have to feel in yourself you have worth," he answered. "Friends, family, a loving relationship, um, just because we are human, and that's how we're built. . . . These are all reasons to stay around."[2]

Dawkins agreed with everything Gervais said, and they are not alone in the belief that our biology directs us to seek out a meaningful life.[3] Many atheists—in fact, I think it's probably safe to say most atheists—believe both that we need a meaningful life and that it is possible to obtain one. And we don't need God for this. According to Dawkins, that would be childish:

> There is something infantile in the presumption that some-body else (parents in the case of children, God in the case of adults) has a responsibility to give your life meaning. . . . The truly adult view, by contrast, is that our life is as meaningful, as full and as wonderful as we choose to make it. And we can make it very wonderful indeed.[4]

So, what makes life wonderful? What is our purpose? Well, perhaps the best, at least the wittiest, answer comes from the late Christopher Hitchens. When asked what the purpose of life is if God doesn't exist, he said, "I can only answer for myself; what cheers me up: gloating over the misfortunes of others."[5] In the context of the debate he was in, it was a wickedly funny answer that may have been quite true for Christopher, for all I know. His wit was a gift, and he used it here to make the point that finding purpose—something to cheer you up—in the absence of God isn't really all that hard. Sam Harris said the same thing in a less dramatic way:

*What is the meaning of life? What is our purpose on earth?*
These are some of the great, false questions of religion. We
need not answer them, for they are badly posed, but we can
live our answers all the same. At a minimum, we can create
the conditions for human flourishing in this life—the only
life of which any of us can be certain.[6]

What Harris and his counterparts argue is that it doesn't
take a holy book to know that we prefer pleasure to pain.
Therefore, let's create a world that limits pain and allows
people to construct whatever life is meaningful to them
according to their preferences. This is our bare minimum
purpose, and it's more than enough to guide us in a scientific pursuit of a meaningful life.[7] We can come together
and, through a rational process, agree on the things that
really matter in life. There are always going to be outliers, "people who don't get the point of it or go their own
way," as atheist philosopher and cognitive scientist Daniel
Dennett describes. But as long as they don't hurt us, "we
can let them be."[8]

On the surface, this position does seem liberating just like
the young college girl said. It does feel grown-up in a sense.
Because life has no inherent purpose, you are not bound to
another's plan or design. Life—your life—is a blank slate
awaiting you to create a story of meaning and value. Don't
obey God. Be a god. Make your life as meaningful and wonderful as you want, however you want. You don't need to
inherit a meaningful life; you can create one for yourself.

If you find meaning in writing books to help others, write
books. If you find meaning in devoting your life to winning
games, play games. If you find meaning in relationships,

pursue whatever kinds of relationships seem right. If you find meaning in isolation, be alone. Become a counselor or one who gloats over others' misfortunes; it doesn't matter. Whatever cheers you up, whatever gets you out of bed, whatever is your reason to stay around, it's all good. Follow your heart. Be true to yourself. It's your human right to determine your own path. It's what you do. Just don't hurt anybody.

Well, it's not that simple.

First, we all know plenty of people who spent their entire lives pursuing the things they found meaningful, obtaining them, and still feeling empty. Many have even given their lives to noble causes and succeeded in killing the world's demons, only to find their personal demons alive and well. It's quite a trite thing for someone to tell you to just follow your passions and you'll find meaning. Seriously, what world do they live in? Nearly every week, people who have it all kill themselves. How's being true to yourself really working out?

Second, when it comes to finding meaning in life, are we simply looking for something that makes us feel as though our lives matter, or are we looking for something that actually tells us that our lives matter? This is the whole point the college girl was making. It is nice to be free to do whatever we want as long as we don't hurt anybody, but why is what we decide to do worth anything? Having the freedom to pursue whatever we think makes our lives meaningful is only good as far as we have the ability to convince ourselves that our feelings are a good judge of our lives' meaning. Are they? Is feeling good about what we do what makes our lives meaningful? If that's the case, we have a problem bigger than simply the personal struggle to convince ourselves that our lives matter.

## The Problem of Morality in a Meaningless Universe

Why *shouldn't* I hurt anyone?

"Should" implies purpose, what we ought to do. But if life is inherently meaningless, if there are no rules beyond what we make, why should I care about your suffering even if I don't want to suffer myself? Why can't my meaning include your misery? In an inherently meaningless universe, it would be incorrect to say that humans are supposed to experience happy and joy-filled lives, and therefore we ought to limit pain and suffering. We are not created for any purpose. There are no "shoulds" and "oughts" regarding our existence.

At best, all we can say is that we don't prefer suffering. But not preferring something, even cruelty, isn't the same thing as it being objectively wrong. I don't prefer vanilla ice cream, but I don't think you should be locked up for serving it to me. Well . . .

No, of course you shouldn't. We don't call the violation of mere preferences evil. For something to be judged objectively wrong, truly immoral, and evil, it has to violate some kind of purpose, some kind of standard that goes beyond subjective personal or group preferences. And so the question is, What makes us think that the arbitrary standard we create out of a meaningless universe is worthy enough to be this kind of judge? And why does it deserve anyone's obedience?

What if I don't like the rules we make? As selfish as that sounds, what reason to be moral could be given to me beyond an appeal to my own self-interest? When my preferences come into conflict with your preferences, who settles the issue? Say I am a cruel man, and I enjoy exploiting the weak. It gives me purpose and meaning to rid the world of what I consider to be a lower form of humanity. I delight in it. Or maybe I'm not cruel necessarily. Maybe I am morally motivated to rid the world of life forms that I think rob the majority of a greater happiness. Maybe I'm Thanos.

One reason I love the Marvel film *Infinity Wars* is because it's philosophically engaging. Thanos, the villain in the story, is morally motivated to create a net gain of happiness for the universe by killing half the living creatures in it. He is a true utilitarian.[9] But why is he a villain? Why shouldn't he snap out five trillion souls if it results in the greater happiness of an untold number of people both now and in the future? Thanos is not wickedly motivated. At least he doesn't conceive himself to be. He thinks he is the savior. He is willing to sacrifice his life to do what others are either too morally inept to see or too weak and cowardly to carry out. And if there is no purpose to human life other than creating happiness for the greatest number of people possible, Thanos is the tragic hero of the story, not the villain.[10]

You might say, "That's ridiculous! You can't just hurt others."

Says who? A group of people who got together and developed a social contract based on the principle "If you don't hurt me, I won't hurt you"?

Okay, say I won't hurt you. Instead, what if I'm like philosopher David Hume's Sensible Knave, and I just let all the weak abide by this social contract while I worked it to prosper at your expense?[11] What if I did it without you even knowing? What if I found a way to make you believe that you weren't really suffering from my exploitation? Would I be doing anything wrong? How would you answer that? What could "wrong" even mean in a universe lacking purpose other than going against the self-aware preferences of the majority?

There is a real problem here. There is no motivation for me to go along with the arbitrary rules of the majority outside that of self-interest. But if self-interest is the basis for how I make moral decisions, then what happens when my self-interest directs me to go against the rules? How will you persuade me?

And don't try to tell me that things are just better for everyone when we work together. That may be true if I need you, but if I can find a way to prosper at your expense, good luck convincing me otherwise. You have told me that my life is only what I make of it, to listen to my heart and be true to myself, and that I am free to construct a life of meaning of my own choosing. If there is no transcendent standard for life, if I am not accountable to anything other than my interests, then what moral weight could our social contract really have? You have just written the origin story for a generation of supervillains. Let's hope most are cowards or too dumb to figure out there aren't really any rules.

This would be an absurd world, a world where meaning and morality are reduced to preferences deemed acceptable by a majority. It would be a world filled with inherently meaningless lives declaring inherently meaningless actions meaningful because they feel good and are acceptable to the majority. And it would also be a world where power is the highest good. Where there is no purpose, one needs power to create a world that reflects their preferences and to stop those who threaten those preferences. In this world, we are all villains.

This is the epitome of vain existence. But it gets worse. What about human value?

## The Problem of Value in a Meaningless Universe

Remember, in an accidental universe, human life is not intrinsically valuable; it's functionally valuable. Human beings are not valuable by virtue of what they are; they can only become valuable by possessing certain characteristics that make human life a valuable means to an end. So what are these necessary characteristics to obtain value?

It is commonly argued that personhood, not human nature, gives life moral worth. *Personhood* is defined as the state of being able to immediately exercise the capacities of rationality, self-awareness, and desire. The list of characteristics that constitute personhood is sometimes longer, but you typically won't find a shorter list than this. The basis of the argument is that the ability to be aware of your existence and make rational plans for pursuing desires makes your humanity worth something. Without personhood, a human being is merely flesh and blood.

Think of the argument this way: If you are not aware that you are alive and you do not want anything, can you actually be harmed? Is anything really taken away from you if you aren't aware that you exist? Is there even a "you" yet? And if nothing can be taken away from "you" in any meaningful sense, then what thing of value could your life possibly possess?

This reasoning is why it is commonly argued that the unborn lack moral worth.[12] At their stage of human development, they have not obtained the ability to immediately exercise their natural capacity for rational thought. As such, they are not aware of their existence, nor do they desire one. They are human, and their human nature will naturally give rise to rationality and such if it is not affected by things like trauma, disease, or premature death. However, at this stage of development, they do not possess the necessary characteristics that would enable their human body to be a valuable tool for obtaining a desired end.

Straightaway, though, I'm sure you can see a problem with this position regarding human value. All human beings have a natural capacity for rational thought, self-awareness, and desires because of their human nature, but they might not be able to immediately use those capacities because of trauma, disease, disability, stage of development, or even sleep. If the status of personhood is conferred on the basis of your ability to immediately exercise the capacity of rational thought and desire, then you lose personhood. Every night for several hours, "you" cease to exist, as does your aunt in a coma, your elderly grandmother, your unborn child, your newborn child, and perhaps your daughter and my son and all those with cognitive disabilities.

So why prefer this concept of personhood as the source of human value and diminish the value of some human beings who, through no fault of their own, do not possess these characteristics? The answer is that we have to if human life isn't valuable in and of itself and can only be a valuable means to a preferred end. In this kind of world, if we cannot use our humanity to pursue something of value, then our humanity is worthless.

## The Inequitable World of Extrinsic Value

Though this concept of personhood may be the only choice for human value in an accidental universe, this choice is deeply problematic. It destroys our hope for human equality and creates an enormous burden for us in the pursuit of personal value.

First, rationality, self-awareness, and desires are degreed characteristics. They are not things that either you have or you don't. They are things that develop over time and can change. Think about it. At what point in life do we become rationally aware of our desires? Further, are we all equal with respect to our rationality and the awareness of our desires? Of course we aren't. So how can a degreed and emerging property of human nature be the thing that grounds human value and equality? In other words, if the things that give us our value develop and change, it stands to reason that our value develops and can change.

Not everyone is equally rational. Not everyone is equally self-aware. Not everyone equally has the desire for life. And think about that last one. If the desire for life is part of the basis for conferring personhood, then what happens when that desire goes away? What about the suicidal? It would seem we are morally obligated or at least morally permitted to take their life rather than help them. Is that the world we live in?

Second, personhood as commonly defined cannot be valuable in and of itself. In an accidental universe, rationality, self-awareness, and desires are not intrinsically valuable; they are functionally valuable. These characteristics are only valuable insofar as we are able to use them to gain something else of value—namely, the fulfillment of our desires. They thus cannot be the basis of human value. They only allow us to obtain something else of value.

Personhood in this sense cannot be any more valuable than human nature. In a universe of extrinsic value, human nature is functionally valuable because it gives rise to personhood, and personhood is functionally valuable because it enables us to pursue desires. The real thing of value, then, is the end, the fulfillment of desires.

But what happens if I am never able to use these characteristics effectively enough to achieve any kind of desirable end? Does my life really have any value? If I am never able to obtain any of my desires, what was the value of my rationality and self-awareness? Functionally, they were worth nothing to me. What good is it to have a tool with which I fail to produce anything worthwhile, no matter how hard I try?

So I'll grant you that rationality may be valuable, but I am not. My rationality and self-awareness did not produce anything of value for me. They are more like a curse than a gift. All I am is flesh and blood that is painfully aware of how pathetically empty my life is. In a world of functional human value, I'm not sure how you could argue that my life of unfulfilled desires is worth anything. I am still nothing more than flesh and blood. If the unborn are worthless because they do not have desires, what makes my life of unfulfilled desires worth more?

The quest for a meaningful life in this reality would be terribly burdensome. It would be a world where we are always under the pressure to fight for our desires, because the fulfillment of them is our life's purpose and the source of our value. It would be a world that honestly looks very similar to the one we presently live in, with growing depression and anxiety, increasing violence and hatred, arrogance from accomplishment, and despair from failure. Regardless of which reality is the real one, it seems everyone has chosen to embrace the atheistic one.

If this reality is the real one, we don't matter. Our competency of fulfilling our desires does.

## The Quest for Meaning Is Meaningless without God

Before we end this chapter, let's be sure we have grasped the futility of the atheistic position. If God does not exist, your life is a blank slate without purpose or value. It has the chance to become valuable if you can construct a life of fulfilled personal preferences—but not any personal preference, only the ones that the majority are willing to accept. Even if you were to succeed in constructing a life of fulfilled personal preferences, all it could mean is that you have succeeded in doing what you want to do. Your life would matter simply because you say so and others were willing to go along with you.

If God doesn't exist, that's the best we get. That's our only hope for a meaningful life, and it is a vain hope.

So whatever satisfies us becomes our life's purpose? Whether it is fighting oppression and seeking justice or creating miniature figurines of all my neighbors in our parents' basement and singing to them? It would seem so. Both of these preferences are equally meaningful in a universe of no meaning.

More than absurd, this reality would be terribly burdensome. Ever present would be the thing of value—the career, the relationship, the accomplishment—yet it would be just out of reach for many. Knowing that your life could amount to something but never actualizing it, while being surrounded by others who did, would be a hellish existence, and an inequitable one at that.

This would be a world where some human lives became valuable and others would never succeed in doing so. Our belief in equality would be irrational, and our pursuit of equality would be just another example of pretending. It would be a make-believe reality that likely wouldn't last long. There would be some who would grow up and quit playing along. Why continue to treat people as equals when we know they aren't? Why show respect to people who are standing in the way of our fulfilled desires?

Whether you are a Christian or not, this is the world I think most people live in. This is why you struggle with racist thoughts. This is why you hate Democrats. This is why you are pro-choice. This is why you are thinking about ditching your wife. This is why you struggle with self-worth.

In a world of functional value, human lives are simply a means to an end, the end of fulfilled desires. And if someone doesn't have desires, can't fulfill their desires, or is robbing us of our fulfilled desires, what good is their life? In a world of constructed meaning, what use do we have for people who get in the way of the world we are trying to create? There is none. We simply need the power to get rid of them.

This is where we are headed. At least, it is reasonable to think this is where we are headed. Everyone wonders how Germans could have exterminated those who got in their way. It is because of the thinking that human life is only functionally valuable. It is because of the belief that some lives are unworthy.[13] It is because evolution has taught us that whatever allows for the survival of our species is good.[14] And it is because if there are no rules beyond what we make, then any clever and powerful man can do an awful lot in the name of reason.

Or we can embrace a different reality. The reality I believe is the real one. The one where your life is valuable regardless of whether you can pursue your desires, obtain your desires, or even have desires. In this reality, *you* are valuable, not your ability to do something, earn something, or create something. *You* matter in this reality, not because inherently meaningless lives got together and decided that your preferences were okay to pursue. No, in this reality you matter because of what you are, but I suspect you already know that. Now it's time to find out if that belief is a true belief and where it came from.

# 3

# God and a Meaningful Life

Have you ever known someone to give themselves their own nickname? I had a friend in high school who wanted us to give ourselves nicknames. I laughed and thought he was joking. But no, he was serious.

"Come on, call me 8-Ball," he said.

"Ha! No. What does that even mean?" I asked.

"Come on. It's cool. You can pick one yourself."

"No. That's stupid. I'm not calling you 8-Ball. Maybe if you were a pool shark, and there was an epic story of how you hustled some guys out of some money in a sketchy bar or something. But I've never even seen you play pool. 8-Ball doesn't mean anything."

"It doesn't have to mean anything. It can just be cool."

"Uh, okay, whatever you say."

I never called him 8-Ball. I don't think he ever got anyone else to call him that either. But even if he had, all he would have succeeded in doing is getting the rest of us to go along with something entirely meaningless because he liked it.

Such would be all of life if God does not exist. There would be things that we call meaningful and maybe even get others to go along with. But inherently meaningless lives don't suddenly become meaningful just by declaring that their inherently meaningless actions are meaningful. We could pretend our actions and lives matter, but we would always know the truth.

The atheistic quest for meaning is thus deeply problematic. Meaning must precede an action for the action to be truly meaningful. It is kind of like nicknames. We don't just go from non-meaning to meaning out of nothing. Meaningless things cannot just declare something meaningful and thus it is. There must be something objective for an action to correspond to in order for it to be either good or bad, meaningful or not. There must be a standard, and that standard must be something far greater than our feelings or the arbitrary preferences of a majority.

Fortunately, we do not live in an absurd universe. Life is inherently meaningful and human life is intrinsically valuable because God exists. He is what grounds meaning and value. But what exactly does that mean, and does it really make any practical difference in the quest for a meaningful life?

"How does that reality actually change anything for me?" you might say. "I've always thought God existed, and I still feel worthless." Fair enough. It's time to explore inherent meaning and intrinsic value a bit more and see if truly understanding and believing this reality changes anything.

## What Am I Worth?

Have you ever struggled with your self-worth? Most people have. Why did you struggle? I imagine it was because there was something lacking from your life that you believed made your life worth something. Perhaps it was a relationship, an accomplishment, or a characteristic like beauty, intelligence, humor, or athleticism. I imagine there was a conflict in you. On the one hand, you would deny that those things are what give life value. On the other hand, it was the absence of those very kinds of things that made you feel worthless.

It's important to note that when someone struggles with self-worth because they do not possess some characteristic or some accomplishment, their struggle has its root in a particular view of life. And it is an atheistic view of life. Those thoughts in your head about why you're not worth anything or not worth as much as so-and-so are not based in reality. They are lies. Why are you believing them?

Do you believe that your value comes extrinsically from things like relationships, accomplishments, and certain characteristics like beauty, intelligence, and athleticism? If you're honest, you'll likely say no and, well, yes. And that's okay. Much of life is a struggle to know and believe what's real.

I imagine you reject racism, sexism, homophobia, and all unjust discrimination. And you rightly do so because of a conviction that all lives matter and are equally valuable. Yet I also imagine that you have your own personal ranking of people who are more valuable than others—people with certain looks, certain careers, certain abilities, and certain accomplishments. They have things you lack that you might be jealous for and that make you feel worthless or inferior.

So which is it? Either it is time to admit we believe in a functional view of human value and cast away our desire to believe in equality, or it's time to embrace the view that all lives matter because of what they are and not because of what they can do. And if all lives are equally valuable because of what they are, it is because they are intrinsically valuable, and that can only be if God exists.

## Our Intrinsically Valuable Lives

We are valuable by virtue of what we are because we are made in God's image. The Bible does not mention the image of God much. It is only explicitly mentioned three times: Genesis 1:26–27; 5:1–2; and 9:6. In these texts, the Hebrew words *tselem* and *demuth*, respectively translated as "image" and "likeness," are used to show that we are in some sense like our Maker.[1] Our nature is sort of a shadow, a representation, a likeness of God. It shows our unique relationship to God among other created things and the unique way we reflect his glory. It also serves as the basis for why we are not to shed the blood of another innocent human being (Gen. 9:6).

Exactly what the nature of this likeness is, we are not told in the Bible.[2] There is a certain ambiguity to the concept. Though we do not know fully what being made in God's image means, we are told what really matters: because of what we are, we are loved by God and reflect his glory in a unique way.

Think about that. Your nature was created in a way such that God's glory, what God is like, is revealed in you. What more dignity could you possibly have? And more than what you are, you are loved. You are loved by God, the being of ultimate worth, goodness, and wisdom. He knows you. Every bit of you. And yet he loves you.

This love was most clearly seen in the fact that he died for our sins. Before you or I even had a thought about God, either to love him or to hate him, Jesus Christ was going to give his life as a ransom in order that we might be reconciled to God and brought into his family as an adopted son or daughter (Eph. 1:3–14).

So what are you worth? You bear God's image, he loves you, and he has made a way for you to know him and abide in his love forever. You could not be worth more.

Maybe that sounds cliché to you. Maybe you are worn out on this idea because you have seen too many highway billboards or signs at football games. But really think about what this means. God needs nothing, lacks nothing, and is totally sufficient in himself. God's love is entirely unconditional. You are not needed; you are wanted.

His love for you is rooted in his holy nature and not your actions, your characteristics, your accomplishments, your successes, or your failures. You are and always will be loved by God, and in this, God's glory is manifested and your value is secure. To the weak and the broken, this is good news. To the proud, it might be bad news. But our value does not belong to what we will do or what we have done. We are valuable because of who God is and what he has done.

## The Significance of Our Value

That human nature is unimaginably valuable does not diminish the value of God. I bring this up because some mistakenly believe that unless we think that human beings are the scum of the earth, we cannot have a proper view of God. But it does not follow that just because we recognize the value of humans, we therefore must have a lesser view of God. Our value is derived from him and is a reflection of his great worth. Having a high view of our value does not depreciate God's, any more than appreciating a priceless painting devalues the painter.

I think the misunderstanding stems from believing that unless we think little of humankind, we will not think rightly about our sin, and we will somehow conclude that what we have done really isn't that terrible. However, I think only when we have a proper view of God *and* humans will we understand and hate sin for what it is. Humankind does not need to be ugly in order for God to be beautiful.

It is right to hate sin, but that is where our hate must remain. Self-hatred is not holy. Sinners need only to repent and be cleansed of their sin. They do not need to spend the rest of their life minimizing their significance.

We are allowed to feel good about ourselves. There are plenty of things we have all done that we should feel bad about. There will even be some sins for which we will feel the sting of regret and shame for the rest of our lives. That's okay. It means we have a heart.

What we have all done has condemned us, and rightly so. We have hurt others, and worse, we have sinned against God. We should feel the full weight of our actions. But in Jesus Christ and the forgiveness he alone offers, that condemnation is no more (Rom. 8:1). He forgives us because of his grace, and he renews us such that we can carry out the good works he has prepared for us. We are his workmanship (Eph. 2:8–10). What a thought.

The simple idea here that you may be struggling to believe is that even though you have done terrible things, you are still loved. You are still valuable. You still have work to do that God has prepared for you. You are not unworthy of the riches of God's grace any more than the rest of us. Yes, you will feel bad for what you have done. That's life. But your feelings do not condemn you. Draw near to Jesus, for there is nothing that can separate us from the love of Christ (Rom. 8:31–39; Heb. 4:16). Remind your feelings of that truth and live in the freedom that was bought for you with the blood of Jesus Christ.

You may not feel valuable, but you objectively are. That's way better than merely *feeling* valuable. Of course, feeling worthwhile is a gift, but that feeling will come and go over the course of your life. And when it goes, know that your value has not left with it. Challenge your feelings with true reality, and enjoy the gift of peace that comes with embracing what you are and what you are worth.

This reality is the great equalizer for those who struggle with pride and despair. Some of us look at all we have done and become arrogant and proud. Some of us look at the lack of what we have done and become anxious and depressed. All of us need to look to the Lord and at what has made us all equally valuable. This reality should bring humility to the proud and hope to the broken.

At times in my life, I've been on both sides of this. I have known arrogance, and I have known the anxiety that comes from thinking my life isn't worth much. But being intrinsically valuable means that we never have to worry about creating a life of value. Our anxiety and arrogance are misplaced.

This reality changes everything. We cannot make our lives any more valuable than they already are. But we can waste them.

## Our Objectively Meaningful Lives

What are we supposed to do with our valuable lives? What were we created for? In short, we were created for God's glory. This purpose is quite amazing and easily misunderstood.

The word *glory* means honor or a recognition of something for its great worth, and some think that we were created because God needed someone to tell him how good he is. Human existence in this view is a patronizing existence, as the point of our lives would merely be to stand before an insecure king and feed his vanity.

I can understand the source of this misunderstanding. We often project ourselves onto God, but God is not like us. He is a maximally great being. He has no deficiencies, no voids that need filling. Though we may need others to tell us how great we are, God does not. He was content in and of himself without us.

So why did God create us then? If God doesn't need anything, why bother making us at all? I think the reason is love. I can think of no greater act of love than for a maximally great being to create something that is able to know and partake in his goodness. God's love, not his vanity, compelled his creative act. God did not create us because he needed us to glorify him, but that which God creates can and should do no other.

First, if God, the maximally great being, chose to create something, what would the nature of that thing be? Could God create something with a nature that did not bring him glory? Really think about that. It's a logical absurdity. A maximally great being cannot make something that doesn't display his great worth. And even if he could, why would he? It would be dishonest. It would be evil and unloving to create something whose intended purpose was to deceive and make God appear to be less than what he is, for it is good when the creation apprehends the greatness of God and wants nothing more than to partake of his goodness.

Second, all created things will, by virtue of what they are, bring glory to God, and we, the part of creation that is aware of who God is, must also choose to glorify him. Works of art bring honor to the artist, and should a painting ever become aware of its beauty, it ought to praise its maker as well.

But it isn't simply a duty to glorify God. Do you understand that to glorify God means that you comprehend, at least partially, his greatness? Glorifying God means knowing who he is and responding in an appropriate fashion. To glorify God, in this sense, is no more a duty than celebrating when your team has won, the band returns for an encore, or your child has accomplished almost anything. It is no duty to rejoice when beholding something worthy of praise.

The objective meaning of glorifying God by knowing and rejoicing in his greatness is sufficient all in itself to tell us that our lives matter. Now, that may not do much for your feelings yet. That's okay. There's more to the story, and there is work for you to do.

## How Do We Live Out Our Meaningful Lives?

The fundamental purpose of our lives, thus, is to bring God glory, but the way in which we do so is dependent on our unique nature, what we are. Stars and mountains and all created things bring God glory, but not like we do. It isn't good enough just to know that we are to glorify God; we also need to know how we do that. Otherwise we might view God as an oppressive tyrant and ourselves as his slaves. The truth is quite the contrary.

Often one begins thinking about God and religion by thinking about rules and law. That's the wrong place to start. Creation is where to begin. In Genesis 1–2, we learn that humans are made in God's image and are given what is often referred to as the cultural mandate: the authority and responsibility to care for the earth (Gen. 1:26–30). God instructed us to multiply, to subdue the earth, and to have dominion over it. We are to use our collective strength and knowledge under God's headship to bring order and beauty to what could be a world of chaos.

Some think the creation account in Genesis is poetry rather than history, and it certainly could be. That wouldn't mean, though, that the creation account is wrong. Poetry and history are not enemies, and however people reflect on what God has made, wonder and worship are appropriate.

Psalm 8 is a poem in which David, the author, reflects on God's creation, rejoices in God's majesty, and marvels at human exceptionality. This psalm captures a contrast. When we look at all that leaves us breathless in this world, we are struck with our relative lack of importance. What are we in comparison to this?

If you've ever stood atop a mountain, gazed at the stars, or beheld the beauty of the vast sea, you know the feeling of awe and insignificance. It is like a joyful dread. Majesty overtakes you, and happiness and fear fill you simultaneously.

You feel as if this thing of great beauty and size could consume you in an instant if it were to give your little life even a moment's thought. This is David's reaction to God and his creation. *Who am I, that the maker of all this should be mindful of me?* But David's awe is not only because the maker is mindful of humans; it's because God has placed them in charge of what he has made.

The cultural mandate given by God is for humankind to rule the earth God created, to cultivate it, and to care for it. Adam's first task was to name the animals. In naming something, as we still do today, we exert our authority and creativity. And that is what God has given us: the freedom to exercise creative authority to care for the world he has made. We are subcreators.

We do not have the ability to make something from nothing, but within what God has made, we have the authority to organize the created and bring forth many new things: medicine, technology, science, art, architecture, agriculture, and on and on. We fulfill this calling when we create a vaccine, harness the power of water or the atom, and build homes and skyscrapers and adorn them with art. We honor God by discovering and using physics, exploring and cultivating new lands, and inventing all sorts of helpful or just plain fun gadgets. This creation is to be enjoyed as well as managed.

I bet many of you never realized that you are glorifying God by studying calculus so that you can build bridges, improve architecture, and predict radioactive decay.[3] Who knew that those who build rockets, create fashion, and care for puppies can glorify God in these acts? It isn't only singing and preaching and tithing that glorify God. It is creating.

Now, there is a right and a wrong way to exercise our freedom. Our creativity is not without confines. There is a moral order to life because God has created things for a purpose. There are standards we should follow. Lines we ought not cross. But this is not oppressive. Indeed, the creative freedom God has given us wouldn't actually be meaningful without purpose. But creativity that has meaning and purpose is extraordinarily fulfilling. And that is the purpose of our lives: to glorify God through the creative freedom and authority to care for the earth he made.

# Creative Love
# and Our Chance for Joy

I have always loved music and sports. Some of my earliest and fondest memories are of my family and neighborhood friends playing football, baseball, and soccer in backyards and cul-de-sacs. Actually, we played anything we could. Whatever season it was, we would find a way to imitate the athletes we saw on TV. Even in Georgia, we found a way to play hockey.

We weren't confined simply to the games of others. My brother, my sister, and I could make a game out of anything while we were growing up. Foilball may have been our best.[1] Not all the games we played were for sheer amusement. We each played sports competitively, and I got to play baseball in high school and college before I traded in a bat and glove for a guitar and pick. And for seven years I got to write, travel, and play music with some great friends. It was an unexpected and joyful time.

Music and sports are very different, but there is something they have in common. Each time a game or instrument is played, there is both order and discovery, rules and creativity. There is a script for each, and at the same time, there isn't. It is in this strange space of new and old where the known and unknown are seamlessly intertwined. And in this tension is excitement, nerves, wonder, failure, and success. It is exhilarating and deeply satisfying, and yet it still leaves you wanting more.[2]

In the creative process there is freedom, wonder, and the excitement of discovering what you are creating. *What is going to come next? If I do this, what will happen? What if I try this?* Both music and sports have this quality. If you've ever been in a locker room or backstage after a concert, you have heard the joyful and congratulatory words of discovery and accomplishment, the words every six-year-old has said: "Did you *see* that?"

Whether you are a musician, an athlete, or neither, you know the experience I am describing. Creativity is not confined to arts and sports. It is in the way we talk to one another, pursue the love of our life, bake bread, solve problems, and raise our kids. All of life is creative. Creating seems to be what we were made to do, and in creation we find great joy.

We might be tempted to think that it is the freedom in creativity that is satisfying. Freedom is part of that, but it is not the whole. Freedom needs some kind of gravity for it to be useful. Creativity needs borders, a canvas. Even abstract art has order. There is a big difference between paint flung on a canvas and paint flung all over your living room. The joy of creating is made possible because it exists within boundaries. Creativity without order is just chaos, and that is not our calling. We are to create out of chaos.

Imagine a gathering of musicians where each musician could play any series of notes in any time signature they wanted. Or imagine a gathering of athletes on a field where each athlete could grab any sort of equipment and do with it as they pleased. It would be mayhem.

Now imagine you came off that field and people cheered you and said, "Well done! What a game!"

"What a game? I just spun around in circles and randomly hit and threw stuff."

"Yeah, but you did it so well."

Wouldn't that be absurd? Sports are enjoyable because there are rules and objectives. Music is pleasant because there is order and composition. There is creativity in each, but the creativity is meaningful because it is within some kind of purpose. There is a striving toward an end in both sports and music, which makes both the journey and the arrival satisfying.

Just as we can imagine the absurdity of sports without rules and objectives, or music without keys and time signatures, so we can imagine the vanity of creative freedom without purpose. Where there is no purpose, there can be no success. Try to imagine the futility of life if success is impossible. And I don't mean hard. I mean truly not possible. Success is a meaningless word in a world without purpose. Without purpose, all of our creative effort would be nothing more than aimless flailing and paint splatter.

In an accidental universe containing no purpose, there can be no satisfaction from accomplishment because no standard is ever met. Stuff is just done. Even if you assign meaning and create purpose, all the joy of creation in this kind of world would merely be the satisfaction that comes from being good at something for which you made up the rules. Create a game, win that game, give yourself a trophy, and be proud of yourself if you want.

If life has no objective purpose, that's as good as it gets. But that is a sad life, a life of pretend accomplishments. A truly meaningful life is one filled with the freedom of creativity and the joyful discovery of accomplishing something of transcendent purpose. It is filled with choices that actually matter in the pursuit of accomplishing something of true significance. It is not simply being the MVP of Foilball.

But just as you can imagine the absurdity of a world with no purpose, I'm sure you can imagine the misery of a world without creativity. This would be a world where you were forced to follow rigid rules to produce predetermined outcomes. That would be as pointless a life as the one where success was never possible. What makes life truly meaningful isn't merely that there is transcendent purpose—robots could possess that. It is that we are free to create within that purpose. And that is the kind of world God made, a world where we are free to creatively love.[3]

## The Meaning of Love

Love as we know it is many things. We are right to say we love sports, food, places, and people. But not all love is merely strong affection. There is also romantic love, the feeling of transcendent bliss. It is the feeling that no matter how close you get to your love, you are still not close enough. It is like you want to become one with another, and it is beautifully intoxicating.

Love as we know it has a benevolent quality to it. When we love something, especially a person, we are concerned with the goodness of the object of our affection, not simply what we can get from it. Love is an intrinsic good. Its goodness isn't based on its ability to produce something good for us. Love is not merely a means to an end.

Love is a disgusting idea when stripped of benevolence. Without a benevolent quality, all that love can represent is the affection I have toward things I benefit from. It would be transactional in nature. That would be a perverted and grotesque notion of love. It would mean that what we feel toward each other simply represents what we get out of each other. But people are not a means to an end. The love and affection I have for my wife and children are not simply representative of their usefulness to me. At the core of love is others, not myself.

If God exists, then love of this kind can exist. Love is a part of God's essential nature, and this love is pure. It seeks the good of others without malice, greed, envy, selfish ambition, or any other selfish impurity (1 Cor. 13:4–7). That is the nature of love, and God has made his love known to us both through his actions and by giving us his Spirit. We know this love because we are loved by God (1 John 3:16; 4:7–21).

If God does not exist, the feelings of love ranging from affection to romance are nothing more than an adaptation for survival. Love is merely chemical reactions interacting with my flesh. It came to exist because of an evolutionary process that has allowed my species to survive. It is good only in the sense that it allows my kind to go on. It is pragmatic and selfish at its core. I feel the way I do toward you because it is advantageous for me to do so. The reason for love is survival.

There's no way around that. Without God, the Creator and Sustainer of life, benevolence can't exist, at least not how we think of it. For even when we feel as though we are acting unselfishly, it is merely a pragmatic illusion of evolution. Our biology has tricked us into thinking we are doing something benevolent, but what we are really doing is good for each of us and our kind in the long run. If God does not exist, love is not love like we know it, and we need to embrace a colder transactional reality. We should all have written different wedding vows:

> "My love, I have for you an irresistible biological urge caused by chemical reactions that are the result of an evolutionary process that allows for the survival of the fittest. Whether it's you or someone else, I am programmed at an instinctual level to feel this way in order that we might procreate and ensure the survival of our species."—Your genetically engineered and socially programmed biochemical mate

If God does not exist, one of the best things in life does not exist like we think it does. But because God is love and he has loved us, selfless love exists and can be experienced. Knowing this kind of love determines the nature of our relationships.

## The Meaning of Relationships

Because love is not self-seeking at its core, relationships are not utilitarian. We do not use people for what we can get from them. Rather, we are able to seek their good ahead of our own and enjoy friendships and romance without strings.

Friendship is another intrinsic good. We can delight in other people for who they are and not merely for what they can give us. And the reason we can do this is because we know the love of God. He who gave his life as a ransom for ours loved us by dying on the cross for our sins. We who have experienced love like this can surely love others.

There is no more noble purpose in life than this: to know the love of God and love others as he has loved us. Again, it's wrong to view God and religion through the lens of rules. We do not have to love. We *get* to love and be loved. And we are free to love creatively. It is the primary way we steward the creation.

Many of you who have fallen in love know the creativity that love sparks. When my wife and I were falling in love, we drove all night to sit on a beach for one hour, then we grabbed some Krispy Kreme donuts at three a.m. before driving back to go to class. Well, she went to class. Anyhow, want to guess how I proposed several years later? It involved planning and distracting—okay, lying—and creating a way to get her back to that beach with her thinking it was her idea. It worked, by the way.

The marriage of love and creativity is pure bliss. But creative love isn't only relegated to romance. Many of you know the experience of going out of your way to care for someone else. That is love. When you plan a going-away party, that is love. When you devise a way to comfort or cheer up a friend, that is love. When you invent new ways to say "I'm sorry," that is love.

Creatively loving others is what you are made to do. It's why you feel so good serving others. I know that is a bit presumptive of me. But I'm right, am I not? Some of the most fulfilling experiences in your life came from serving.

It was that time you risked your reputation and your nose to stand up to the cool kid in high school. It was that time you gave that poor man something to eat. It was that time you stopped what you were doing to talk to the girl everyone made fun of. It was that time you sacrificed your vacation to spend a week with your friend in recovery. It was all of those times you put your needs second. How opposite of what we would think. Life is found by giving it away.

We were made to love others, and the creative ways in which we love are limitless. Understanding this changes another fundamental part of stewarding creation: work.

## The Meaning of Work

A life of creative love is central to our purpose, and it changes the way we view everything, including our work. Work can be tiresome and unfulfilling, an enormous burden to carry. It is especially burdensome when we have accepted a functional view of human value. I know of many men and women who feel worthless because they never secured the kind of career they thought they would. But we do not work to earn value; we work because we are valuable.

Many choose careers because of the presumed value they will add to their lives. But we must always remember that what we do does not determine what we are worth. Rather, it is precisely because we are all equally valuable that we lovingly serve each other through what we can do.

In a Christian worldview, there are not sacred and secular callings. All work is to the glory of God; it is a means of having dominion over the earth and a way to creatively love your neighbor. So pursue a career as a doctor not because it will add dignity to your life but because you want to love your neighbor and see the sick made well. Pursue a career in law not for the relative significance society will give you but because you love your neighbor and want to see the weak and the marginalized protected. Pursue a career in politics not for the power it brings but because you love your neighbor and want to see that all people are free to live out their inherently meaningful lives.

And embrace the freedom to leave your career to serve others if it's needed. Raise your children with all the dignity a life of love is due regardless of what society or your parents will tell you about staying home. Let others define their significance in what they do if they want. You are made in God's image and are free from the shackles of needing others to validate your calling. Go love creatively, and whatever work you do, do it for the glory of God, not the esteem of others.

## Creative Love and the Chance for Joy

I don't know what you think about God and life. Some think that God and religion are meant to rob people of real happiness. Many have described God as an oppressive tyrant out to kill joy and enslave humanity, and religion, at best, is like opium used to keep us in place and make us settle for a hallucinogenic happiness, not a real one.[4] The exact opposite is true. God, the author of life, made us capable of enjoying him and the world he created. There could not be a more meaningful and free existence than the one where we get to creatively care for God's creation with others while enjoying the loving presence of the One who made it all.

Every part of life is an opportunity to live out our noble calling. This is why we are told that whatever we do, we should do it for the glory of God (1 Cor. 10:31). This is a radically freeing thought. It means that our potential joy is not dependent on our circumstances. Wherever life has us, whatever life has done to us, whatever dream has been shattered, this day, we have the chance for joy.

Joy is another one of those elusive concepts. What is it? Well, it's a good feeling, an emotion, not an idea. It's not happiness, but it's very much like it. In a way, joy is deeper, richer, and more satisfying. It's like a happiness in your soul. It's not the laughter that comes from a joke; it's the feeling right after, when you look at all your friends around the campfire who made you laugh, made you cry, and stood by your side when you needed them the most.

Joy is like total satisfaction. I think this is the fulfillment we are all chasing. Since it is a feeling, its presence will be felt more acutely at times. But there is a kind of joy that is so satisfying that the feeling is almost always present if we are paying attention and diligently working to keep other things from stealing it. Now, because joy isn't an idea, we can't simply decide to be joyful. But we can fight for it.

I believe the pursuit of a meaningful life is the fight to find the joy that comes from abiding in Christ and living out the purpose for which we were created. Jesus asks us to abide in him so "that my joy may be in you, and that your joy may be full" (John 15:11). The way we abide in Christ is by keeping his commandments (v. 10). That makes sense. If God created the world and designed it a certain way, wouldn't following his commands lead us to discover the joy we were meant to find?

Now, just so you don't misunderstand me, I'm not saying you use Jesus to get joy. Rather, I'm saying that joy is found by embracing what you were made for. And you are made to know God, experience his presence, and, under his leadership, fulfill your calling to creatively love and care for his creation.

So repent of your sins, turn to the Lord, and abide in him, and may you experience the times of refreshing that come from his presence (Acts 3:20). Choose this day to follow him, cultivate the land you are living in right now, and find the joy that comes from embracing your noble calling to care for this earth by creatively loving others as yourself.

I don't mean to say everything is going to be okay instantly. Some of you are in really dark places. Some of you have been living pretty rough lives, maybe as the consequence of your own choices. There are many things that can bury your joy. The rest of this book is about those things. And there perhaps is no greater joy stealer than hating who you are. So let's consider how being made in God's image changes the way we view our identity, and how that leads to joy.

# 5

# The Joy in Our Identity

Cultural catchphrases often do more harm than good. Whatever they begin as, they usually end up being nothing more than sound bites that oversimplify life and don't really mean what they say. Take "Just be true to yourself," for example. What does that mean? How do you do that? What if you don't know who you are? What if you don't like who you are? Say you are an angry and violent person, or timid and insecure, or maybe lazy and prone to procrastinate. What if you are a combination of all these nasty traits? Should you still be true to yourself? I don't think any of us would say yes.

We all know that person who thinks they are the smartest one in every room and needs to make sure others know it too. If you don't know that person, it might be you. And if you have ever said, "Hey, this is just who I am—I tell it like it is," after offending everyone in the room, you are definitely that person. We'd rather you not "be yourself," by the way. Your intellect is not a license to be an intolerable schmuck.

Perhaps I'm being too literal with this catchphrase. We all know that our identity is not a blank permission slip for our behavior. Maybe I'm also being a bit too harsh in my critique of it. There is a reason the expression "be true to yourself" exists. Knowing who we are and living accordingly is a big deal. We all need an understanding of our identity and what it means.

So, who are you?

## The Importance of Knowing Thyself

When someone says, "Tell me about yourself," where do you start? What do you say? Of all the things you could talk about, what comes to your mind, and why do you suppose you thought of that first? Do you start with your career, your faith, your family, your ethnicity, your sexual preferences, or your gender? What about a characteristic like athleticism or intelligence? What about what's in your bank account? Goodness, I hope not. Nobody likes people who define themselves by how much or how little money they have. So what did you think of first? Is that who are you, and why does it matter?

It's the last part of that question that's really important. Who we are matters, doesn't it? We've heard of people having an identity crisis. Maybe you've had one yourself. We've taken personality tests, looked to horoscopes, and partaken of all sorts of psychological trends designed to help us "know thyself." We do this because there is security and purpose in knowing who we are. When we don't know who we are, we feel like a ghost, a phantasmic soul aimlessly drifting about with no greater goal than to haunt others and make them share our misery.

Maybe you've felt this emptiness after a breakup or divorce, or after the loss of your job, a specific ability, or your beauty. Maybe you feel it now as you come to the middle of your life and find that everything you've been working toward has been for nothing. It feels like you're lost, doesn't it? Not knowing who you are is a lonely place of both being unable to make sense of the past and not knowing what to do next.

I experienced this sense of homelessness at the end of my days as an athlete. It was the summer after my junior year in high school, and I was at the Olympics in Atlanta watching a baseball game between Mexico and Japan with my youth minister, Carey Hudson. (I wonder if he remembers this story.) During the game he leaned over and said, "Mike, you know this doesn't happen to me often, but yesterday while I was reading the Bible and praying, it felt like the Lord was telling me something about you."

"Okay . . ."

"I think he was telling me that you're not going to play baseball your senior year."

Ha. Yeah, right. But what was eerie about this was that I had already begun thinking that the Lord didn't want me to pursue baseball. I was good, not great, and I was getting some interest from colleges. An MLB career was probably not in my future, but I thought coaching might be. Still, I knew the Lord was leading me away from something that was very much a part of who I was. It was an unsettling idea.

Why would God give me this ability if I'm not supposed to use it? If I'm not an athlete anymore, who am I?

Well, Carey—or I guess I should say the Lord—was right. I didn't play my senior year. I ruptured a disc in my back and failed two classes, and though I would have tried to tough out the season, academically I was forbidden. The next several years of my life aren't the ones I'm the proudest of.

I struggled to know who I was and what to do with my life. I failed out of college twice, and a junior college at that. I picked up some destructive habits that took some time to get rid of, but I did not abandon God, and he did not abandon me. I did end up playing a season of college baseball, and I am grateful for that experience, but back surgery wasn't required this time for me to learn what I needed to learn.

During this wasteland of irresponsibility, I had one of the most humiliating experiences of my life. I'll tell you that story over a drink and a good meal, but not here. I will tell you that in my humiliation God convinced me of something I have been fighting to believe ever since: my significance is not found in what I do; it is found in what I am.

I suppose it's time to move past the importance of identity to its nature. Let's see if we can sort out the complexities of this subject and see how the existence of God affects who we are.

## What Is Identity?

When it comes to identity, we are talking about the things that make me "me" and not you. There is a Mike Sherrard who is unique—thank God—and not like anyone else. I am an individual who is an amalgamation of all sorts of things.

My identity consists of experiences, abilities, accomplishments, interests, values, beliefs, and more, as does yours.[1] This is a fairly common understanding of identity, though simplistic, held by both psychologists and philosophers, and it is compatible with a biblical worldview.[2] I don't think there is anything in this understanding of identity that is unhealthy or untrue.

What makes me "me" and not you is a number of things. There is nothing wrong with being identified as an individual in this manner. If somebody asks you, "Who is Mike Sherrard?" it is perfectly reasonable for you to say that I am a Christian man, husband, father, pastor, writer, speaker, and a number of other things. If you know me well enough, it's not wrong for you to include my personality traits, my habits, my temperament—be they good or bad—and even my nationality and political beliefs. I am all of these things.

Where identity becomes a problem, though, is when we latch on to the wrong things and allow them to become the essence of who we are. We often reduce our identity to certain beloved parts of our identity, and those become the sum total of who we are. The tragedy, of course, is when the things that we believe truly define us go away—and most things do go away—who we are is lost, as is our significance.

Beauty fades. Relationships end. Jobs are lost. Failure is part of life. What we are good at might become irrelevant to others, or we may lose the opportunity to use our gifts. And there is nothing much worse than being good at something but being unable to do it. It is hell. Not much is permanent, and if what defines us and our significance has an impermanence to it, we should expect a vicious life cycle of finding and losing ourselves, obtaining something of significance and losing it, and never really knowing who we are. Many of us are in this cycle. It's time we got off this rat wheel.

But we can only get out of this cycle if God exists.

## The Significance of God's Existence for Our Identity

A self-aware genetic mutant is the essence of who you are if evolution is your creator. Anything beyond that is up to you.[3] If God does not exist, the meaning of your identity can only be found in the value of impermanent things—the combination of desirable characteristics, experiences, abilities, accomplishments, and so on. So grab on to the things you like best, and let them define who you are and what you are worth. That's all you have. Best of luck making something of yourself. Hopefully you will like who you become. The essence of who you are is in your hands.

But if God exists, things are the exact opposite. Your essence is the result of his hands.

A human being loved by God and bearing his likeness is the essence of who you are if God is your Creator. This is the core of our identity, and it is the greatest defining thing about us. Anything beyond that is like a beautiful frame adorning a priceless painting.

In thinking about who we are, it is right to think in hierarchical terms. There are some parts of our identity that are more important than others, and understanding their importance puts things in perspective. This is true whether God exists or not. Whether I have black or brown hair isn't as important as whether I am a male or female, which isn't as important as whether I am made in God's image or am a cosmic accident.

When we think about who we are, it would be foolish to start with the lesser things. Who is Mike Sherrard? Well, I wear a size 12 shoe, have a crown that is wearing away on my right front tooth, and have disproportionately short arms. Now, that's an absurd way to conceive of myself. Maybe not to you, now, and especially not to my friends. I will forever be known this way by them.

But the absurdity of conceiving of myself by beginning with my shoe size is equally matched by the absurdity of beginning with anything other than the fact that I bear God's image. All the parts of our identity, the things that make us "us," are still very meaningful. But they pale in comparison to the dignity that comes from being made in God's image. That is the quintessence of who we are, and to exchange that for something else is really quite ridiculous.

Terri and I try to help our kids understand the essence of who they are by the way we praise them. My children are beyond special to me. And it's not because of their hair color, their intellect, their goodness (which they often seemingly have none of), or any other thing that makes them who they are. So, when I praise my daughters for their beauty, I tell them I would love them the same if they were as ugly as a witch. When I tell my boys I'm proud of their courage and toughness, I tell them I would love them the same if they became a supervillain. (I also tell them I would hope Superman would defeat them, but you get my point.)[4]

My kids are all different, and their differences are meaningful. They are what make them unique persons. But it is not their uniqueness that makes them special. There is no quirk or gifting they could possess that could rival the simple reality that they are my kids. Succeed or fail, love me or hate me, their value is ever fixed because they are mine. I want my kids to live in the security of who they are, knowing that their value is separate from what makes them unique.

By analogy, we can begin to comprehend our significance if God is our father. If we, who are often bad parents, can value our children simply because they are our children, how must a perfect heavenly Father think of us? Surely what makes us important is not our abilities, our achievements, or anything else. Our differences are only like jewelry adorning the face of a child already beheld as beautiful by a loving dad.

Central to who we are is who he is. We are different, and we are special, but what distinguishes us cannot compete with what we have in common. It is upon this reality that we can begin to construct a proper understanding of our individuality. But before we look at our uniqueness, we need to consider one more thing that we can have in common.

## Identity in Christ

The Christian catchphrase "My identity is in Christ" is often used with little more thought than the secular catchphrase "Be true to yourself." Even so, what it means is incredible. We must note, though, that one does not grow in value by becoming a Christian. However, belonging to Christ is either an incredibly important part of our identity or something we need to consider.

To say my identity is in Christ is to say that because I belong to Jesus, there are several things that are true about who I am. Because I belong to Jesus Christ by responding to his call and placing my faith in him for the forgiveness of my sins, I am no longer condemned by my sin. I am clean, set free, released from my bondage, filled with the Spirit of God, and awaiting an inheritance as a child of God. I am able to live by his power to resist and to overcome the brokenness in me and in this world. I am one who is forgiven and accepted by God. This is who I am in Christ.

You may be a fearful person, but in Christ you have been given a spirit of power (2 Tim. 1:7). You may have a disability, but in Christ you can endure hardship (Phil. 4:13). You may be an addict, but in Christ you have been set free from the bondage of sin (Rom. 6:15–23). You may be fatherless and an orphan, but in Christ you belong to his family and have a countless number of spiritual brothers and sisters (Rom. 8:12–17). And again, most importantly, you may be one worthy of condemnation because of what you have done, but there is no condemnation for those in Jesus Christ (Rom. 8:1). If God has justified you by your faith in Christ and his atoning sacrifice, who is there to condemn you (Rom. 8:31–39)?

How remarkable that in Christ we can become the righteousness of God (2 Cor. 5:21). When you think about who you are, let this be in the front of your mind. This is either a hopeful and unbelievably true thing about you or something that can be yours today. Call out to God. Today can be the day your sin is exchanged for God's righteousness (Rom. 10:9–10).

That we are in Christ doesn't negate the other meaningful things about us, but it does put them in their proper place. In a hierarchical understanding of identity, being made in God's image and belonging to Christ are powerful truths that provide clarity for the way we view the other aspects of our identity. They will guide us and allow us to joyfully embrace who we are and live out a meaningful life. They will help us to be proud of who we are without becoming prideful, to lose good and bad things without losing ourselves, and to see and celebrate our differences.

## Being Proud without Being Prideful

There is a misunderstanding of humility that insists that to be humble you must never think you are good at anything. That is nonsense. You are not prideful and arrogant simply because you know you are good at something.

Delight in the fact that God has made you in such a way that has allowed you to work hard and develop good things in your life. Be the best at what you are good at, but do not strive for success because you need the validation that comes with it. Rather, be the best because of your desire to honor the God who made you and because you want to love your neighbor with your gifts. And if you do become the very best in the world at something, you can leave pride and arrogance behind because you still do not possess anything that is more significant than what anyone else has. All are made in God's image.

So be proud of your accomplishments. Be proud of your traits. Be proud of your relationships. But do not be so proud as to foolishly believe that every good thing in your life is the result of your hands. Remember all good gifts have their origin in our sovereign God. And don't be so foolish as to exchange the honor that comes from being made in God's image for the honor that comes from lesser things. Your identity can become an idol if you let it.

Think of parents who try to live out their dreams through their children. Maybe they never became what they thought they would, and now their identity is wrapped up in making something of their kids' lives. If their kids succeed, then they are known as the parents of someone great. This quest for an identity to give them significance becomes an idol they are enslaved to.

This temptation isn't only relegated to the vicarious ambition of parents, of course. When we find our significance in the good things about ourselves, in addition to becoming prideful, we all become slaves to our identity.

For example, if what gives my life significance is intellect, I must be known as the smart guy. I can never be wrong, everyone must know that I am smart, and I will spend my whole life fighting for that. I cannot afford for others to not know who I am because my relevance is attached to my intellect. This idolatry does not allow for me to be humble. I must always get the last word. I must always dominate conversations. People must always agree with me on everything, because if I'm not the smart one, what am I? What's so special about me?

Do you see how knowing that the source of my significance isn't in something like intellect allows me to resist pride and be truly humble? I can be proud that I'm smart, but I don't have to be known as smart. I can be wrong. I don't have to get the last word. I can use my intellect to help others feel smart even if it makes me look dumb. Whatever others think about me has no bearing on my significance.

## Losing Something without Losing Ourselves

There are a number of good and bad things that we all need to let go of. This can be hard if these things have become central to who we think we are. However, if we have a healthy understanding of our identity, should we lose something good, be it an ability, a relationship, or a characteristic like our wit, we can be sad, but in our sadness we can know that what we have lost isn't the essence of who we are.

If you have the ability to do something and it is taken away from you temporarily or permanently, you are allowed to grieve its loss. Athletes who must throw in the towel are allowed to be sad about it. But they can let it go, because the essence of who they are doesn't go with it. If you have lost your health or your job, you are allowed to grieve your inability to provide for others. It is hard to be cared for. But your dignity isn't found in your ability to provide.

For the successful, the wealthy, and the fulfilled, you are free to lose it all. Many of you work endless hours, have sacrificed one relationship after another, and substituted satisfaction in lesser things for fulfillment in God. Remember, you are not the one who earned your value and your significance. It is yours because of what you are, not what you have accomplished.

Likewise, for the divorced, the disabled, and those in the midst of failure, know that you have not lost what makes you significant. You have certainly lost something meaningful, and it is perfectly fine to grieve that. But take heart. You are not defined by what you have lost.

Also, just as you can let go of good things, you must let go of bad things. Many of you identify yourselves by your worst mistake. It has become who you are, and it is like a heavy chain holding you down. Maybe you've been told over and over that you are nothing more than your worst mistake.

Well, it is not who you are. It is something you have done. You can leave this part of you behind.

Replace the evil thought that you are what you have done with the knowledge of what God has done. He has made a way for all your worst deeds to be atoned for in Jesus Christ. The Lord has not allowed your worst mistake to define your life, so don't you allow it to either. Look to the cross of Jesus Christ and be reminded of God's greatness, his glory, and the fact that while you were still an enemy of God because of your sin, he died for you. You have punished yourself long enough for what you've done. It is time to seek forgiveness, follow Jesus Christ, and leave your sin behind. It is not who you are.

Lastly, and maybe most importantly, others do not get to define who you are. Maybe you've grown up with someone who told you that you're nothing. That you're ugly, fat, a stupid piece of _____, and someone nobody will ever care about. Maybe they explicitly said this every day or communicated it subtly over many years. Whatever the case, leave it behind. Their judgments mean nothing. They hurt, for sure. May God graciously deal with them for the pain they've inflicted upon you. And may he even grant you the mercy to be able to look at what they've done and forgive them. Either way, you move on. You are not what others say you are. You are what God says you are.

## Seeing and Celebrating Our Differences

In attempting to avoid racism, some people will say they don't see color. But they do. And they should. People of color are beautiful, and our diversity is something to be happy about. We all should cherish our heritage while knowing it isn't the greatest thing about us. This ought to give us the freedom to see, hear, and learn from people not like us, and to celebrate what makes them "them" and not us.

Those who are not like us need to be seen. The disabled, for example, need to be looked at. I have a son with a rare genetic disorder. He needs to be seen. I have friends who have children with Down syndrome. They need to be seen. You know what I'm talking about, right? Whether it's someone missing an arm or possessing an extra chromosome, you want to look but feel like you can't. So you awkwardly avoid looking their way. Whether you mean to or not, your actions convey pity. They don't need your pity. Our children bear God's image just the same as your Little League all-star does. What they need is to be seen.

Diversity is good. Division is not. In humility, a beautiful unity can emerge out of our diversity. Let us together embrace that our significance doesn't come from what makes us different but rather from what we have in common. And what we have in common is infinitely more valuable than our differences. Our nature brings glory to God, and we are free to lovingly and creatively serve others with whatever our unique gifts, ethnicities, abilities, gender, experiences, and desires are.

## The Joy in Embracing Who We Are

I can embrace the fullness of who I am—quirks, flaws, and everything—and so can you. The good things we can take pride in, care for, and develop for the glory of God and the good of others. The bad things we can change and leave behind. And the parts that we have no control over, we can grieve, accept, overcome, and be filled with joy about, for we are not the sum total of our parts.

Maybe you've been told you are ugly. So what? Let vain people live in their vanity and find their value in something as impermanent and petty as their looks.

Maybe you are failing in your career and are constantly reminded of it by your neighbor, who can't stop flaunting his importance at work. So what? Let your neighbor feel good about being the assistant to the regional manager and the little power he has while he has it.

Maybe you are lonely and every day have the relationships of others paraded before you through social media. I won't say "so what" to this. Being lonely is hard. But you are not an undesirable loser or something gross no one wants. You are a man or a woman dressed in the honor of God. You are his image bearer, and you are loved by him. In him is the ultimate satisfaction our lonely souls seek. So in your lonely times, draw near to Jesus, and may he fill you with his presence and bring you good friends, and maybe, in good time, even the love of your life.

I could go on, but I'd better rein it in before I get too sappy or my sarcasm gets me in trouble. It's quite sad, though, and fair to mock the exchanging of the honor that comes from being made in God's image for the honor that comes from lesser things. We are far more than what we often reduce ourselves to, and we should make fun of ourselves for doing so.

Therefore, let us abandon the pursuit of finding identity in relatively trivial things and begin to live securely in the reality of what and who we are. Our uniqueness is not what makes us special but is a gift nonetheless. Let us each consider, then, the ways we can encourage one another to use our uniqueness for the glory of God and the good of others. And let us see how who we are might affect what we are called to do.

6

# The Joy in Our Calling

The alarm didn't go off. Or maybe it did and you hit snooze, half awake. Either way, you are going to be late unless everything goes your way. Which of course it doesn't. Your keys hid themselves while you were sleeping, the traffic lights conspire against you, some inconsiderate jerk decides to get into a wreck and hold up the freeway, and just because life wanted to give you the middle finger, your parking spot is blocked due to some pointless construction and you have to park three blocks away. This is the third time being late this month, and two of the times weren't your fault, but the boss won't care. His boss doesn't care. All the corporation cares about is results. Work sucks.

But it's not supposed to. Work is good. It is part of our purpose. It was given to us before the fall of Adam and Eve.

There is great joy in building, inventing, curing, solving, teaching, caring, growing, fixing, and protecting. We would do these sorts of things even if we didn't get paid, because it's what we were made to do.

God could have made the world such that it ran on autopilot and we were always provided for miraculously. But he didn't. Our dignity is such that God uses us to see that his creation is cared for and its needs are met.[1] This is part of our purpose, and it's why we can love to work. So why does our work often become the bane of our existence? Well, there are at least three reasons.

First, though work is part of God's creative design for us, it will be toilsome as a consequence of sin and the brokenness in this world (Gen. 3:17–19). Even though there is joy in it, it will still be work, not play. Don't listen to those people who say to just do what you love and you'll never work another day in your life. Nonsense. There is a grind even to the work we love. Playing with puppies all day still means you have to clean up their, well, you know.

Second, though what we do matters, it can become why we think we matter. When work becomes what determines our significance, it is going to make us either really prideful when we succeed, stressed out when we are climbing the ladder, or depressed when we fail. When work becomes something it wasn't meant to be, frustration is likely to follow.

Remember, you don't work to earn value; you work because you are valuable and so are others. Work is an opportunity to love your neighbor and steward your unique gifts and abilities for the glory of God. Use it for what it was intended for. Stop using your work to convince yourself that you matter. Rather, work for the good of all who matter.

Third, though many of us like to work, sometimes we end up doing work we are not built for. We pick a career path and realize not soon enough that it isn't for us. But it's not too late. Whether we are just starting out or are many years along, we can discover the unique way we are gifted to fulfill our calling of caring for this creation and loving others in our work. And we can do this by considering our gifts, experiences, and desires in the context of what is needed.

## What Are Your Gifts?

What are you good at? Not what do you think you are good at, but what are you actually good at? Where have you had success in life? Some of the easy places to look at are academics, athletics, financial achievements, good relationships, and the arts. These things give you the luxury of a standard with which to compare your abilities against those of others.

But the really important question isn't where you've had success; rather, what made you successful?[2] It could be that you were successful in sports early on simply because you were the biggest and oldest kid in your league, and you had an unfair advantage. It could be that you got good grades in school because you are incredibly smart or that you have an unbelievable work ethic. The same goes for finance. It could be that you had a number of friends because you were attractive, not because you were a great listener and a kind person. It's not enough to simply recognize where you have succeeded. You must ask why you were successful in order to discover what your gifts are.

For example, I was good at sports growing up, but I don't know that it was due to natural athleticism. That was my brother's gift. He could roll out of bed without practicing for a month and go hit two home runs and pitch a no-hitter. He wasn't lazy. He was just that good. I, on the other hand, would stay in the batting cage until I felt like I had hit every ball perfectly, which is something I never thought I did. My success was more attributed to my desire not to be bad than it was my natural ability to be good.

Also, I had the ability to hear instruction and then put it into practice. I could listen to a coach or watch somebody do something and mimic it quickly. I've always had the ability to comprehend something and then turn it into something useful for myself or others. Growing up, I took great joy in showing the other neighborhood kids how to hit a baseball, kick a soccer ball, or throw a spiral. It was just as satisfying for me, perhaps more so, to show another how to do what I learned as it was for me to do it myself. That is the gift of teaching.

It wasn't just that I enjoyed teaching others to do something, though. They enjoyed it too. I was able to teach them. I succeeded at it. And I knew this both because I saw it and because others told me.

In addition to reflecting on what you are good at, consider what others have said about you. Now, other people do not get to determine what you are good at, but often those around you can see and praise your gifts. They are good at seeing the things you may be blind to, both your strengths and your weaknesses.

As you consider your gifts, take the long view. Go back to your childhood and notice any recurring positive experiences. What do your successes have in common? Do you have a knack for solving problems, organizing, designing, or encouraging?

I discovered that I had a drive and a gift to help others succeed by knowing how to do something the right way. This desire was sanctified by the Lord, and as an adult, I have the same drive and giftedness, but it is a little different. I want to know what is true so I can help others find life in Jesus Christ. This assortment of gifts made me good at playing baseball and helping my friends get better at it too. Now I use these gifts to help my friends win a different sort of prize (1 Cor. 9:24–27).

## What Are Your Experiences?

The past is a prologue. Often what comes before us shapes and directs us in what is to come. This is not determinative, of course. The past does not bind our future. But it is right to consider how our experiences meaningfully contribute to our ability to do something good in this world.

In addition to your gifts, what have you experienced that has shaped you in a unique way? What has life taught you? What have you seen? What hardships have you faced? What success have you had? And what does it all mean? In a universe of meaning and purpose created by a sovereign and good God, no pain or experience is gratuitous. What might your experiences mean for your work?

Experiences overlap with gifts and desires. Often they give you new skills and will change your desires by giving you something like empathy. But not all of them are in the category of skill or desire. There is another kind of knowledge that comes from experience. Those who have positions of leadership know what it is like to have the weight of an organization and the lives of their employees on their shoulders.

This is not something you can know until you have experienced it. Similarly, you cannot know what it is like to have a child with a disability. You cannot know the pain of a miscarriage. You cannot know abuse or bullying. There is much you cannot know unless you have experienced it. And these experiences shape you in a way that is more profound than simply learning a new skill or becoming more empathetic.

How have your experiences made you the right person to love your neighbor and honor God in your work?

## What Are Your Desires?

Similar to thinking about where you have been successful, you need to think about what makes you feel alive when you do it. It could be making a meal for friends. But what about that makes you feel alive? Is it the joy of serving? Is it the joy in creating and experimenting? Is it the joy in making the meal, or is the meal a means to the joy of conversation and listening?

Our desires can be complicated. But upon reflection, we can notice patterns. We will see a recurring theme of meaningful experiences that brought life to us. In that reflection, we can home in on what is unique about our desires. We will discover what makes us come alive when we do something.

Another way to root out your desires is to ask not what makes you satisfied but what drives you. Are you driven to defend, bond people together, acquire resources, learn, or experience something? These are all perfectly fine motivations. Of course, how you pursue the fulfillment of those desires can be good or bad.

I'm driven to defend. My sense of justice is what gets me out of bed and keeps me up late at night. I learn, acquire resources, and bond people together so that I can defend. Even when I was young, I was driven by this desire. For example, I would routinely pick the worst kid in football first. I thought it unfair to win just because someone stacked their team, and I thought it cruel for a kid to feel unwanted.

How can your desires be used to serve another through your work?

## What Is Needed?

Often someone will give advice concerning what to do with your life by asking, "If you could do anything regardless of money, what would it be?" Now, if that is asked simply to root out desires, then it's a good question. But it often suggests that the basis for deciding what to do with your life is grounded in what makes you happy.

There are a number of things that bring happiness, and some of them come with little pain. Say you love persuading people of what is true and then mobilizing them for a noble cause. There are many ways you could do this. You could run for political office, become a motivational speaker, pastor a megachurch or a small local church, or join a beloved nonprofit organization that champions the homeless or one that advocates for the unborn. Which option are you going to choose on the basis of "if you could do anything"? I'd pick the life that contains the most reward with the least amount of suffering.

But as image bearers who want to glorify God by loving our neighbors, we ought to think of our work in light of who we are *and* what is truly needed in this world. This is not to suggest that we must choose only that which contains suffering in order to please God. Suffering may or may not come our way. Neither is it to suggest that if we choose more difficult work we possess a more meaningful life. But the consideration of our gifts, experiences, and desires must be done in the context of what is needed.

When we are freed from a life of creating value through our work, we can consider our calling in light of what is needed. This is what allows some moms and dads to leave the workforce to raise their kids for a time. It is what allows a prosperous lawyer to leave his life as an influential politician and start a pro-life nonprofit. It is what allows a creative musician to leave his record label to pastor a small country church. We all need to consider what we must do. Very few get to do only what they want to do. But this doesn't come at the expense of joy. Maybe some happiness, but not joy.

## The Joyful Intersection of Gifts, Experiences, Desires, and Need

You have been uniquely shaped to work for the glory of God and the good of others. In the intersection of your gifts, experiences, desires, and need is a sweet spot. I wonder if you've approached what you do with this in mind. Maybe you chose a career simply for the money, thinking possessions will bring you joy and significance. Maybe you chose a career because of the pressure of your parents and society, thinking that the approval of others will give your life worth. Maybe it's time for a change.

If you are just starting out in life, it is not wrong to make a lot of money and to be in a respected line of work. But do not start with the work; start with who you are. You have unique gifts, experiences, and desires that you can use for the good of other unimaginably valuable people. The freedom and joy you have when this is the foundation for your work are unrivaled.

Even if you are far along in a line of work you are not suited for, it may not be too late to change, but it may not be worth it for any number of reasons. Joy can be had even in a job you regret taking. Within your job, find an avenue for your gifts, experiences, and desires to be used, even in small ways. And remember that not all work is the kind you get paid for.

Often a job gives you the opportunity to use your gifts to serve others. You may hate your job but love how it allows you to be present and provide for your family. This is also one of your callings. You may hate having left the workforce but love the chance to be home and raise your kids. You may be exhausted from your business but love how your profits allow you to be generous to the nonprofits of the world.

The joy that comes from work isn't bound only to what you do from 9 to 5. You have the ability to live out your meaningful life in a number of ways through many different kinds of work. You are a citizen, a church member, a neighbor, a Little League coach, a spouse, a parent, a grandchild, and an ambassador for Christ if you have placed your faith in him (2 Cor. 5:20). There is much work for you to do. And though it is not what gives your life meaning, the meaning in your work is life-giving.

## The Joy from Active Waiting

I want to end this chapter by giving you some advice to help you find joy, particularly in those times of life when you really don't want to be where you are. You may have agreed with everything I said yet are still dreading Monday morning. Well, you may need to change what you are doing. I don't know. But I do know that before you move on to what is next, there is something really important to do. This is advice that has been given to me, and I've seen the fruit that comes from following it. It has helped me find the joy in my work regardless of the circumstances. It has also helped me find what's next. It's called active waiting.

When we are restless, sometimes we just start doing things to get us out of our current situation. But in a universe that contains a loving, sovereign God, sometimes the first thing to do is wait. It is not a passive kind of waiting, though. It is active.

First, be faithful where you are. In discontentment, our eyes move to the future and neglect the present. If you desire for God to use you in a different place, prove yourself worthy where you are. The Lord knows you. He knows what you need. He knows what you desire. So commit yourself to working hard where you are, and trust the Lord to move you on in the proper time. He can bring you the next thing. You do not have to create it for yourself. This is part of active waiting. It will keep you from wasting many years and ruining many relationships.

And here is an important thing to consider. It may be that you haven't learned what you need to learn yet, so the thing you desperately desire may not be good for you at this time. So second, you need to consider that your present situation is a needed experience for what comes next.

There was an invaluable lesson that I learned during a three-year stint in a place I didn't want to be. I'm not sure I could have learned it any other way. Life is full of such experiences. I'm also not sure that I wouldn't have ruined the thing the Lord gave me next if I had not learned this lesson. But I am sure that I would have missed the lesson if my pride got the best of me and my heart became hard. So resist the pride that is telling you that you are too good for where you are. No, you're not. There is likely something to be learned from where you are. Do not miss it.

Finally, I encourage you to talk about your present situation with someone. Find a pastor or a good friend, but not just any friend. Find someone you trust who is where you want to be in life. Maybe they have a successful career, marriage, or ministry. Serve them, learn as much as you can from them, and see if they will help you sort out your discontentment.

Pride often keeps us from doing the simple things that help. And talking helps. Not just any talk, though. Venting to peers may make you feel better, but it likely will accomplish nothing else. You will be right back in the same place tomorrow, needing to vent again. You need to find someone with relevant knowledge who can help you make sense of what you are feeling and what you want to do.

Maybe you feel like you are failing in your calling as a husband and father. Share this with someone you trust. Maybe you are looking for a career change. Share this with someone in the field you are looking at entering. Maybe you are completely lost. Share this with your pastor.

Allow others into your life and let them help you discover your gifts, your passions, and what your experience might be preparing you for. But don't put pressure on them to figure out your life for you. This is not a seven-step process that works without fail. It is simply a humble gesture on your part that the Lord uses to guide you.

Many times in my own life, someone has said something that in any other context wouldn't have meant a thing. They might not have even realized what they said, but it was the thing the Lord used to tell me what to do.

Simple words often part the clouds of confusion, and wisdom comes in the company of those who love God. Inspiration is a friend of friends. It hangs out when friends gather with the intention of seeking God's will for his glory and the good of others.

So be humble, work hard, and go tell your story. And always remember, you do not work to earn value; you work because you are valuable and so are others.

*So are others.* This idea changes so much. Knowing why we all matter liberates us. It can guide us in loving our neighbor and working to see that injustice ends. Let's explore how knowing why we matter changes the way we view ethics.

7

# The Joy in Loving Our Enemies

You have heard that it was said, "You shall love your neighbor and hate your enemy." But I say to you, Love your enemies and pray for those who persecute you, so that you may be sons of your Father who is in heaven. For he makes his sun rise on the evil and on the good, and sends rain on the just and on the unjust. For if you love those who love you, what reward do you have?

Matthew 5:43–46

What a ridiculous idea. Why should I love my enemies, and why would God care for the unjust? Why not just kill them— starve them out by withholding the rain and sunshine for their crops? Why not let them get what they deserve? Well, the answer is really quite simple.

We are all unjust. We have all wronged others and sinned against God. If God did not send his rain on the unjust, it would never rain, and we would never have the chance to find forgiveness. So praise be to the God who is slow to anger and abounds in mercy (Ps. 86:15). And if he loves those who are his enemies, as we all were at one time, we should love our enemies like we have been loved (John 13:34; Rom. 5:10).

This is a powerful idea that slowly changed the world. In our modern sensibilities, we often forget how cruel the ancient world was. But where did these sensibilities come from? Tom Holland, a brilliant writer, historian, and atheist, says they came from Christianity. In his fascinating and ambitious book *Dominion: The Making of the Western Mind*, Holland shows how our morals and values would have been alien in the first century. The world that birthed Christianity was a violent place. Enemies were hung on crosses as spectacles for all to see; slaves were used to build empires and provide sex on demand; women were considered inferior to men and treated as tools that took care of the household and, like slaves, the lust of men; and babies, especially girls, were regularly left outside or thrown down drains to die. It was a world where "the marble fittings, the tinkling fountains, the perfumed flower beds: all were raised on the backs of the dead."[1]

All people clearly weren't considered equally valuable, and enemies were ones to hate and conquer, not love and pray for. The idea to love your enemies was radically countercultural. But this remarkably powerful idea, rooted in the understanding that all people possess intrinsic value and are loved by God, slowly changed the world. The ethical implications that flowed from the cross changed Western civilization. It was like a depth charge, an explosion beneath the foundation of the world, that shook everything up. We are still feeling its ripple effects today. But those ripples are slowly going away. The waves have hit the shore of secularism.

## Ethics Unplugged

In his "Parable of the Madman," Friedrich Nietzsche famously declared that God is dead, and we are all his murderers. The parable, though, is not a celebration of the success in destroying belief in God. It is a mockery of atheist hubris and a recognition of the struggle of replacing one's worldview with another.[2] Nietzsche was intellectually consistent, and he foresaw the challenge that lay ahead for a society that attempts to replace a Christian ethic with another kind. In *Twilight of the Idols* he wrote:

> If you abandon the Christian faith, at the same time you are pulling the *right* to Christian morality out from under your feet. This morality is *very* far from self-evident: this point needs highlighting time and again, English fat-heads notwithstanding. Christianity is a system, a synoptic and *complete* view of things. If you break off one of its principal concepts, the belief in God, then you shatter the whole thing: you have nothing necessary left between your fingers.[3]

Objective moral facts and values fit nicely in a worldview that contains a morally good and holy Creator; they are orphans, though, in an atheistic worldview. Nietzsche recognized that abandoning belief in God, something he believed should be done, was going to break Western civilization unless another foundation for ethics emerged. He pointed out how much the Christian worldview affects one's ethical thinking, more so than the average person is aware.

Nietzsche's rebuke sought to temper the joyful expectation of a godless utopia unless one can offer another metaphysical foundation for ethics that is not simply a Christian one in disguise. And that has not happened. Though secularism may have succeeded to some degree in deposing God from the Western throne, it has done so while borrowing elements of Christianity to keep civilization stable.

Clinical psychologist and bestselling author Jordan Peterson, who as best as I can tell is not a professing Christian, responded to the claim that European secular societies are doing quite fine without God. Peterson quickly pointed out that though secularism is on the surface in these countries, their foundation is a Christian one. He went on to warn, much like Nietzsche, that "we're living on the corpse of our ancestors. But that stops being nourishing and starts to become rotten unless you replenish it. And I don't think we are replenishing it. We're living on borrowed time and are in danger of running out of it."[4]

George Orwell, the famous author of *1984* and *Animal Farm* and an atheistic prophet of sorts, saw this too. In his brilliant essay "Notes on the Way," he laments the success of removing God from society:

> For two hundred years we had sawed and sawed and sawed at the branch we were sitting on. And in the end, much more suddenly than anyone had foreseen, our efforts were rewarded, and down we came. But unfortunately there had

been a little mistake. The thing at the bottom was not a bed of roses after all, it was a cesspool full of barbed wire.[5]

In the essay, Orwell described the violence of the modern world and how people lacked a compelling reason to live as brothers and sisters after their heavenly Father's death. He wrote that people became soulless by abandoning belief in God, and they were like a wasp that had been cut in two but did not realize it was dying because it was eating jam. Orwell offered no hope in the essay but merely pointed out the present predicament created by doing the right thing: abandoning belief in God.

When God dies, other things die with him. What reason do we have to love our enemies and not exploit them? What reason do we have to treat people with dignity and respect beyond self-interest? Fools think the answer to this question is easy. The intellectual giants of old saw the problem. The pop atheists of today would do well to stand on their shoulders.

Now, it is beyond the scope of this book to explore ethics unplugged from God in its fullest. Morals matter, but that is a book for another day, perhaps. I bring this up, though, simply to acknowledge what few seemingly do. We owe our free and equitable world to the Christian ethic of love for our neighbor and our enemy. Christian ethics is the fence protecting our yard. We should think twice before we go and pull up the fence posts.

Rather than tear down what brought forth our world, I think it is time to embrace the love that flows from the cross. Since God loves all people equally, we must too. And surprisingly, love for our enemies brings great joy. Hatred rots us.

## The Ethical Implications of Love for Today

This is a morally confusing time to be alive. However, understanding why we matter can bring us some needed clarity on three of the biggest ethical challenges facing us today: racial injustice, abortion, and sexuality. More than thinking rightly about these issues, though, I think knowing why we matter will help us love those who disagree with us. And our world needs the healing that can come from our love for our enemies.

I imagine you have a hard time not viewing those on the other side of these issues as your enemy. And whether it is right to call them your enemy or not, you are still to love them. Now, loving someone does not mean agreeing with them. In fact, the way we love someone is often by disagreeing with them.

My father and mother loved me when they disciplined me. My coach loved me when he told me the way I was fielding ground balls was wrong. My friend loved me when he told me I was trusting money more than God. And my wife must love me the most, because she is always telling me what I'm doing wrong. (Sorry, that was a bad joke. Love you, Terri!)

Love does not equal acceptance of ideas or behaviors. In many cases that would be unloving. But to love them in your disagreement, you first need to understand them. Our passionate ignorance of these topics is the kindling for our hatred and the disastrous conversations we have all been part of. However, when we grow in knowledge and talk respectfully about these issues, even in the midst of disagreement love can replace our hate.

Now don't think that love simply means telling someone they are wrong. Love means doing what needs to be done to see that needs are met, fellowship is restored, rights are protected, and healing comes to those beaten by the robbers of the world.[6] Jesus loved in both word and deed; he was full of grace and truth (John 1:14). That is our goal. Jesus is our example. Let us love in word and deed like him. Let us lay down our lives for this world. And may our sacrifice turn this world upside down.

The cross was the most visible symbol of Rome's power to oppress. Now, because of Jesus and those who follow him, the cross is the most visible sign of love and sacrifice. It's time for that kind of radical transformation in our world.

So let's see how love for our neighbor influences the way we view racial injustice, abortion, and sexuality.

## Clarity for Racial Injustice

Racism is evil. God shows no partiality. He does not favor one color over another, one cultural heritage over another, or anything else over another. God is the God of all.

Straightaway it is easy to see why the hatred for one group of people on the basis of something as arbitrary as where they come from or what they look like is evil. It is hatred that mocks God. Indeed, racism is a hatred that is a direct attack on God. Because of what men and women are—creatures made in God's image—we are to treat them with the appropriate dignity and respect. An attack on a person is in some degree an attack on God. Hating our neighbor is hating God just as much as loving our neighbor is a means of loving God (Matt. 25:31–46).

Our shared human nature and the respect that should be given to all who possess it is the basis for our belief in equality. The concept of *imago Dei* has changed the world.[7] It alone provides a suitable justification for our belief in equality.

Understanding the source of our significance helps us to realize that what we have in common is far greater than our differences, as meaningful as they are. Cultural and ethnic heritage is both good and bad. There is much that belongs to our ethnic group that is unique and should be preserved and celebrated. But we must be careful. It is possible that in constructing a world that reflects us and our values, we portray the idea that our ethnicity is superior.

Consider one simple example. Was Jesus white? No, not unless he had a condition no one ever mentioned. He was a Middle Eastern Jew. What is the impact of a white Jesus in paintings, sculptures, and art all around the world? I don't know. It would be hard to measure such a thing. But even if it is not done with malice, it is the kind of thing that can communicate that there is something morally superior in being white. These are the kinds of things we all must think through, and we must be careful about creating a world in our image that belittles the image of others.

Just like with our personal identities, the source of significance for our ethnic identities does not come from the sum total of its parts. This gives us the freedom to change or leave behind something like a white Jesus. Even if it hurts because of the sentimental or historic value, we are free to let it go. For our value as a people group is not defined by heritage.

The first Jewish Christians had to leave much of their cultural heritage behind in order to love their gentile (non-

Jewish) neighbors and break down the cultural barriers that prevented true fellowship. Likewise, many gentile converts gave up certain freedoms like eating nonkosher meat in order to destroy anything that might prevent the bond of friendship.

This is the attitude that Christians must have today. I know your defenses are up because many are calling you a racist for simply being a Christian or being white. But you are strong enough to resist the names people call you, and you can listen to the cries of your Black brothers and sisters and see if there are cultural barriers that you need to help tear down.

This thinking also goes the other way. Just because there is something in an ethnic group's past that offends you doesn't mean you have to destroy it. Your significance isn't determined by the mistakes of others in their past. This allows you to be gracious and forgiving. And whether this means that images of White Jesuses should be destroyed, Civil War statues toppled, or Aunt Jemimah replaced, I don't know. I do know that a proper decision is more likely to follow a proper disposition that allows for a good conversation. And that is what is desperately needed today: respectful conversation.

As those who recognize that everyone possesses an equally valuable life, we should listen to each other and work together to ensure that our societies do not unfairly discriminate on the basis of, well, anything. Wherever we find clear examples of unjust discrimination, we should all rally together, protest together, and do what is needed together to see that our laws, our institutions, and our cultural practices treat all with dignity and respect.

Now, we must be discerning in how we go about this. Not all ideas are equal, and not all ideas about how to create a racially harmonious world are good. There are going to be many who seize this moment to create a world in their image. Not all who champion racial injustice do so for the good of their neighbor. We should all be concerned about the influence of unbiblical Marxist ideologies undergirding social theories like critical race theory and the organizations that embrace them. We will not like a world built upon these ideas.[8]

Equality does not equal sameness, and privilege is not necessarily an evil. Let me give you an example before you dismiss me as a racist. I grew up with two parents who loved me in a rather economically stable environment. This allowed me to take risks in life, as the furthest I could fall was back to my parents' home. Even now, should I lose it all, my mom and dad, or my in-laws, would welcome my family and me back home. That's the furthest I, my wife, and my five kids can fall, and it is a soft landing.

There is no doubt that this family structure is a privilege for me, and one I wish everyone to have. But is this an example of "whiteness," as some would say, a characteristic of systemic oppression perpetuated by those in power?[9] Is the nuclear family consisting of a mom, a dad, and their children an inherently racist institution that needs to be toppled? It's hard to imagine, but some believe so. We should be wary of those who, in the name of racial justice, wish to "disrupt the Western-prescribed nuclear family structure" and destroy something good for the sake of equality.[10]

This is why we must be allowed to reason together on this topic. Many of us may be championing a movement without any understanding of the philosophies driving it. We think we are doing something right, fighting for a noble cause, but

we may be unwittingly advancing ideas fundamentally opposed to God's Word that will lead to even greater suffering.

This cannot continue. Christians, we must lead the way.
Our heritage is one of grace and truth. Jesus is the preemi-
nent example. Let us, like him, love and speak truth boldly
and seek to end racial injustice without destroying many
good things along the way. Be the ones who create safe places
for the oppressed to be heard, be the ones willing to suffer for
righteousness, and be the ones who can guide the way forward using the Word of God as our lamp, not the vile trash
of history's villains who have already hurt the world once.
Be discerning and be loving. This is our way.

## Clarity for Abortion

It is on the same basis of seeking the just treatment of all
races that we ought to seek justice for the unborn, provided
they are human in the same way we are. If the unborn are
human beings made in the image of God, then they are our
neighbors deserving the same dignity, respect, and protec-
tion that other image bearers have. So, are they like us?

In answering the question "What are the unborn?," we
turn not to religion or philosophy but to science. We often
hear the claim that the unborn are nothing more than a clump
of cells, and thus they are not a human being. Well, science is
settled on this. The nature of the unborn is not up for debate.

The unborn are not something different in kind from
human beings.[11] The science of embryology has shown that
from the earliest stage of development the unborn are distinct, living, and whole human beings.[12] "Distinct" means the
embryo is not part of its mother, though it is in its mother.

"Living" means the unborn grows and develops, and dead things simply don't grow. And "whole" means the embryo contains all of the genetic information to direct its own development internally. It is not constructed by an external agency like its mother. This set of criteria is why there is consensus in the scientific community regarding the humanity of the unborn.

But are there any reasons why, though human, the unborn do not deserve the right to be protected? Could abortion be justified because of an ethical dilemma, where there is a conflict of competing ethical values? What about if the life of the mother is at risk?

This is where it is important to know what abortion is and why it is wrong. Looking at the pro-life argument as a syllogism, a form of reasoning in which the conclusion is supported by reasons and logically follows from its underlying premises, will help:

Premise 1: It is wrong to intentionally kill an innocent human being.

Premise 2: Abortion is the intentional killing of an innocent human being.

Conclusion: Therefore, abortion is wrong.

Here is why the syllogism is important. In the case of, say, ectopic pregnancy, where the lives of the mother and the child are at risk, you have two options. If you do nothing, both mother and child will die. If you act with the intention of saving the mother's life, you will kill the unborn child. There is no other alternative. Currently, there is no viable medical option to save a child in the case of an ectopic pregnancy. Thus, with the intent of saving the mother's life, the death of the unborn child is both foreseen and unwanted.

By definition, then, is this an abortion? No, it is not. Abortion is the intentional killing of an innocent human being. The intent here is to save the mother's life. Though the death of the child in this case is foreseen, it is not intended. It is an unwanted and regrettable consequence of living in a mortal world where we are often faced with the heartbreaking choice of being able to save only one person. It's as tragic as having to cut the rope of one who is going to pull both of you off the mountain. But it is not an abortion by definition and cannot be used to justify the practice for other reasons.[13]

But what about the well-being of the mother? Maybe the mother won't die, but having a child would harm her in a meaningful way. What if not allowing women to have abortions would set back the women's rights movement? This is a great question. But let me ask you, would you advocate for women to be able to kill their newborn children or toddlers or elderly parents in the name of hardship or women's rights? No? Why not? What is it you assume about the unborn that you don't believe about the other groups?

It is likely that either you don't believe that the unborn are human like us, which hopefully I've addressed, or you don't believe that the unborn are valuable like us. This is why the knowledge of what makes life meaningful and valuable is so important.

If you embrace the idea that the source of human value rests in the fact that we are made in God's image, you cannot arbitrarily decide who to apply that to. As such, because the unborn are human beings made in the image of God, they possess the same sort of worth that you and I do. They only have yet to develop some of the characteristics that you and I have. And though the characteristics—rationality, desires, and self-awareness—are good, they are not what makes human life valuable. Indeed, it is precisely because the unborn do not have them—that they are so weak and fragile—that we ought to protect them even more. Unless we believe that the strong ought to benefit from the weak.

If you have yet to embrace God's existence and the dignity that comes from being made in his image, I challenge you to examine whether your philosophical reasons for killing innocent unborn human beings are tenable. Do you really believe that human value is based on one's size, level of development, environment (the mother's womb), or degree of dependency on another?[14] If you are justified in killing the unborn for these reasons, then you logically must be for infanticide and euthanasia of the elderly, mentally impaired, or medically dependent. But if you are unwilling to pay the intellectual price of your belief, it's time to let it go.

One thing we must not let go of, however, is care for the women and families affected by abortion. Because all lives matter, we must seek to create a world in which every child is wanted and every mother is supported. We must work side by side until all of the societal evils that contribute to abortion are destroyed. But we cannot let our other social justice work salve our conscience and allow us to ignore the legislative reality that allows a million innocent children to die every year. As the great Dr. King once said:

> I am sure you have heard this: "Legislation can't solve this problem, only education can solve it." Judicial decrees can't

solve it, executive orders from the President can't solve it. Only with education and changing attitudes through education will we be able to come to a solution to this problem. Now there is a partial truth here, for education does have a great role to play in this period of transition. But it is not either education or legislation; it is both education and legislation. It may be true that morality cannot be legislated, but behavior can be regulated. *It may be true that the law cannot make a man love me, but it can keep him from lynching me, and I think that's pretty important also.* It may be true that the law cannot change the heart, but it can restrain the heartless, and this is what we often say we have to do in society through legislation.[15]

Just as this was true with the civil rights movement, so it is true with the movement to end abortion. We must seek to change hearts, minds, and the social conditions that make abortion a reality. And while we are working to solve these issues, we are morally obligated to legislatively protect the life of the unborn from the heartless.

## Clarity for Sexuality

Sexuality is a gift. It is a wonderful part of God's design that brings much joy, produces much good, and brings him much glory. It is also something both personal and public. As such, pain and controversy are no strangers to this part of our humanity. We all know someone who has suffered in the quest to understand and live out their sexuality.

Broadly, under this topic are our sexual attractions, behaviors, and understanding of our gender. These are very personal things. They go to the core of our identity. And this is not wrong. Fundamental to our conception of ourselves are things like who to love and how to act in society in light of our gender. This is where the personal becomes public. Relationships are public. Gender roles are public. Our sexuality is not confined to the bedroom any more than we are. People are public, and so is our sexuality.

We don't hear it quite as often now, but years ago we would frequently hear the argument that what one does in their home is of no concern to anyone else. I'm not sure anyone ever believed that. People were advocating for social reform by the very nature of making that argument. Moreover, I think that most people are smart enough to realize that private lives affect public affairs, as we all live public lives to some degree. We go to work, socialize with friends, vote, run for public office, pastor churches, teach children, and coach Little League. We would be foolish to think that our private lives, especially a part that is as powerful as our sexuality, will never influence our public selves.

This is why there is so much fighting today. The quest for a meaningful life includes an understanding of our sexuality and the ability to live it out. And as far as just wars go, fighting to have a society accept what is one of the most powerful and important parts of our lives is worthwhile.

The fight, of course, is tragic. Many lives have been hurt, even ruined. We all know or could tell the story of someone who has experienced a life of hardship surrounding their sexuality. So what is the way forward? Is there anything pertaining to our topic here that can guide us in an understanding of the ethics of sexuality and gender and help us bring healing to this part of a broken society? I think so.

Let's talk about something that may lead to a greater ability to know where each side is coming from and love one another. Christians will often talk in terms of hating the sin but not the sinner. If you are gay, bisexual, lesbian, or transgender, does this language work? Do you feel loved when someone speaks about your life this way? No, according to what many have told me, and I know this is hard for a lot of Christians to understand.

When well-intentioned Christians challenge the morality of one's sexual behaviors, they believe they are challenging those behaviors just as they would any other behavior. When they tell someone they should stop being an angry person, they are not hating that person but are trying to help them. So it's understandable why it doesn't make sense to them when they are labeled as bigots for simply disagreeing with someone's behavior. But here's the issue.

First, presumably there are some Christian bigots, some who do hate the sinner even though they say they don't, and they need to repent of their hateful and unloving actions. Maybe you are one of them or are lumped in with them unfairly.

Second, sexuality is not like the other aspects of our lives. It shapes the understanding of who we are in a much greater way than many other characteristics we have. And this is appropriate. God made us male and female. He made us relational and sexual beings. Our sexuality is a fundamental part of our identity. Telling a man to stop being angry is not in the same category as telling a man to stop being gay.

For example, I am a man who loves a woman. This is fundamental to understanding my identity. If you attack either of those two things, my living as a man or my loving of a woman, you are challenging something at the very core of who I am. It is thus going to be personal and feel like an outright attack on my very essence. In this context, when you "hate the sin," it will feel as though you are hating the sinner.

It will feel like this especially in a time when we have all been influenced by naturalistic thinking. If our sexuality has become the dominant part of our identity, when it is condemned, we will feel as though we are too.

Therefore, greater sensitivity and compassion much be extended when engaging in conversation about this topic. "I'm just hating the sin" is a tone-deaf statement that betrays one's ignorance regarding the magnitude of this issue. It is no small thing to be told that you can't love who you love.

But the essence of who we are is not our sexuality. Our gender does not determine our significance, nor does who we love. Men are not worth more than women, nor married people more than single people. Our sexuality is greatly important, but it is nothing compared to the substance of our nature.

The security that comes from knowing we are God's image bearers allows us to examine all things about our lives, including our sexuality, without the fear of compromising our significance. If meaningful things about our lives need to change, that is okay. What remains fixed is our worth. We are loved by God, and in Christ we have the validation that comes from belonging to his family. We are not alone.

We must submit all things to him, even our sexuality, and ask if we are honoring God with them. Has God revealed his will for our sexuality? If so, what does that mean? Should we reject his design for our sexuality? Is it possible to reject his design without rejecting him? The stakes are high on this one. It would be hard to imagine calling him Lord while rejecting the most fundamental part of his design.

Therefore, if part of your identity is gay, lesbian, bisexual, or transgender, I challenge you to examine God's Word and see if you are abiding in his will. And know this: because God has designed our sexuality, when we conform to his design, though we may lose something we love dearly, we gain the joy of abiding in him.

This is an important topic that we must be free to talk about. I hope it is clear that in thinking that God has a design for our sexuality, one is not necessarily motivated by hate. It can be love that compels them to ask you to consider that the life you were made for is not the one you are living.

And if you are one of those willing to speak such words, be sure you are doing more than loving someone with just your words. Maybe your words aren't needed right now. Maybe you are. Go love one who is weary from this fight. Go love one who has been abandoned by their church. Go love one who has no father or mother anymore. Go stand beside them in their hardship. And may God help both you and them see why life contains hardships for us all.

**8**

# The Joy in Our Hardship

A young man came into my office one morning, and he wanted to talk about his struggle with anxiety and depression. He was a good man trying his best to follow Jesus. He became a missionary, and whereas following Jesus for many doesn't come at much cost, this man knew sacrifice. You couldn't ask or hope for more from a young Christian. So why had God abandoned him?

"My God, my God, why have you forsaken me?" This man borrowed these words of Jesus each night. For years he suffered from severe anxiety and depression. He tried everything to escape it: medication, counseling, spiritual disciplines. And yes, he prayed and had faith. Of course, there were enough people in his life to tell him that he really didn't have faith, for if he did, and just trusted in God more, he would be delivered from his trouble. Job's friends are still alive and well, apparently.

The young man felt like God had abandoned him, but he did not abandon his faith. Ever present, though, was the question of why he should continue to cling to a seemingly disinterested God. Why wouldn't God take the pain away from him? He begged God for relief. He pleaded for mercy. He tried everything to be rid of his torment, yet it remained. Why wouldn't God grant him relief? His doubts about God's goodness grew, and he became almost certain his life did not matter to God. His hardship was the truth.

Can you relate? I'm sure you can. And if you can't, you likely will. This world is broken. None escape pain and disappointment.

I remember listening to this man's story and feeling his despair. I felt quite helpless, unable to comfort or guide. So I prayed, as I always do in counseling situations, as well as when I'm sharing the gospel, defending my faith, or arguing for the goodness of the Christian worldview.

As a brief side note, those who need to know what to say have one who will help: the Holy Spirit. Now, trusting in the Holy Spirit is not an excuse to be lazy. We should learn how to handle difficult situations, answer skeptics' questions, and be ready to give a reason for the hope that is within us (1 Pet. 3:16). But knowing the right answers is not enough.

We don't need a textbook answer when we are sitting with someone in grief because people do not hold textbook beliefs. We need some kind of knowledge that will comfort their aching heart and steady their doubting mind. But we don't know what's in their heart. Are we sure we know what they are really dealing with? Are they? What is truly the source of their pain or confusion? Sometimes it's hard to know. We can guess. We can ask questions to gain insight. But we can also trust the Holy Spirit to guide us. And so I prayed.

In my prayer, a question came to my mind, one that I had never asked anyone before: "Does a meaningful life equate to a lack of hardship?" This stopped the young man in his tracks. His immediate response was, "No." He knew others who had experienced hardship—the loss of a family member, a life of disability, an unexpected betrayal—and he did not think their life was less meaningful than anyone else's. He did not think that God cared less for them or that somehow their hardship was a sign that God had no use for them.

Quickly he realized his problem. He wasn't willing to say that the hardship of *others* made their lives less meaningful, but he did believe that *his* life was less meaningful because of his hardship. It was his very problem with God, what we had just spent the last hour talking about.

And this thinking was understandable. *If God really cared about me, if my life really mattered or had any value to him or others, he would not let me suffer like this. Others don't suffer like me—well, at least not everyone suffers like me. What is it about those who prosper that God loves? Why does he spare some? How did they earn his favor, and why do I receive no help? Why do my pleas fall on deaf ears?*

These are good and fair questions. There is something intuitive about the idea that if you matter to God, if your life was important at all, God would not let you suffer like you are. Love is typically expressed in pleasurable, not painful, ways. But even if you accept the idea that pain can serve a loving purpose, it is very hard to see past your pain to that purpose. When you're in pain, it is only natural to want it to end and to hate the one causing it.

So if you are questioning the significance of your life because of your pain, you are welcome here. It makes sense that you would. Nearly all who experience pain ask these kinds of questions. But what are the answers? Does a lack of hardship mean that God favors you, has blessed you, or has rewarded you for some good deeds or your great faith? Likewise, is pain evidence that God thinks little of you or that you are not as valuable as others? Is it possible to experience joy in the midst of hardship?

It all depends on if pain really does have any purpose. We need a theology of pain if we are going to make sense of hardship in the pursuit of a meaningful life.

## A Reason for Hardship

If God does not exist, then there is no purpose to the cruelty and the pain we experience in life. Again, as Richard Dawkins put it: "In a universe of electrons and selfish genes, blind physical forces and genetic replication, some people are going to get hurt, other people are going to get lucky, and you won't find any rhyme or reason in it, nor any justice." All we should expect out of the cosmos is "pitiless indifference."[1] Without God, pain is gratuitous and as pointless as everything else.

But does the existence of God make things any better? It seems to make things worse. If God doesn't exist, I can easily accept why pain exists. A pitiless universe without any purpose wasn't designed with us in mind. Why should we expect things to go well for us unless we make it so? But if

God exists, and he is good, all-knowing, and all-powerful, why would he create a world filled with so much cruelty, pain, and suffering?

It seems that if God is good, he would want a world without pain and evil, and if he is all-powerful, he could make one. So why doesn't he? Maybe he isn't good. Maybe he isn't as powerful as we think. Or maybe he can't create the kind of world we live in without pain, and maybe there is a reason why.

But wait, he's God. That's out of the question. He can do anything, can't he? It is true that God is omnipotent, but being all-powerful doesn't mean having the ability to do anything. We have all accepted ideas without really thinking them through. We possess certain unquestioned answers, if you will.[2] One of these is the idea that God can do anything. It just seems right, so we don't ever question it. But can God really do anything?

Can God lie? Can God make a one-ended stick, a square circle, or a married bachelor? Can God use his omnipotence to overpower himself by creating a rock so big he can't lift it? Of course he can't, and this doesn't mean that God is not all-powerful. God's omnipotence refers to his ability to do all things that are intrinsically possible and are consistent with his holy nature. God's inability to violate his holy nature or do something as logically absurd as use his strength to overpower himself does not mean his power is limited. Something that is logically absurd does not cease to be nonsense just because we add the words "God can" to it, as the great C. S. Lewis once argued.[3] Therefore, God does not cease to be God just because he cannot violate his nature or do the nonsensical.

So what is it about our world that puts our problem of pain in the category of something like a square circle? Well, it would be our freedom. God cannot create free creatures who are caused or determined to do what is right. Forced freedom is a logical absurdity. Truly free creatures who do not have God's nature will inevitably use their freedom wrongly. It is the price of freedom.[4]

In our ignorance we will make mistakes, be in the wrong place at the wrong time, and create good things that interact with other good things in negative ways. In our moral weakness, we will know what is right but not care. We will desire bad things and make them happen. And in our frailty, we will lack power to always bring forth positive outcomes and to overcome other forces stronger than we are. Because of our nature, if we are truly free, we will create moral evil, cause pain, and be painfully subjected to the nature of this world.

So why did God make us like we are and not like who he is? God is free and not subject to moral evil or mistakes. He perfectly knows all things, desires only good things, and has the power to always enact his will for good. He is a maximally great being. Why didn't God make us exactly like him—not merely in his image but the same as him in every way?

That's a good question, but one that sounds evil in a way, doesn't it? Well, it really doesn't matter how it sounds. It's just as nonsensical as a square circle. This question is asking if it is possible for God to make multiple maximally great beings. But this is a logical absurdity. By definition, there can be only one maximally great being.

So why create finite beings with freedom even though doing so will lead to moral evil and pain? Well, it must be that a world that contains moral goodness is worth the risk of there being moral evil and pain. I think this would be especially true of a world in which you could know and partake of the goodness of a maximally great being. God would be the greatest conceivable good in all the universe. He would be an incommensurate good; nothing could compare to his goodness. Thus, it is very reasonable to believe that all the pain ever experienced would be relatively nothing in comparison to the greatness of knowing God and being able to abide in him.

And isn't this the world he made? A world where we are truly free and able to know him, love him, and abide in his love and life. God has made a way for our moral evil to be atoned for and for us to have eternal life in him. Many of us have tasted this goodness, and we await the full consummation of this joy. Though pain is a present reality, we will one day fully experience God—pure life and goodness itself. And all our pain, no matter how severe, will fade in the light of God's glory and grace.

## What This All Means for the Pursuit of a Meaningful Life

Intellectually, you may know why pain is part of this world, but this knowledge gives you little comfort. It's one thing to deal with this topic in the abstract. It's quite another thing to watch your child die and wonder why God did not stop it. To hell with freedom if this is the cost.

And I understand that. I have a story to tell, one that needs a little more time for me to know how to tell it. But let me just say that I know the difference between the intellectual side of this issue and the personal one. I know what it is like to have nagging doubts about God's goodness and ways. Depending on the pain you've experienced, you may fight doubts all your life. This is normal. This is allowed. God loves skeptics and doubters. And he provides reasons to believe in the midst of doubt. Here are several truths that comfort me in my doubt.

First, I know God knows pain. This is the same world where Jesus Christ suffered and died for our sins. Jesus was both fully God and fully human. And don't simply cast away the pain of Jesus in light of his deity. In some respects, I imagine the pain and suffering a holy God feels is worse than we can imagine. But he does not only know pain. This is the same universe in which God raised Jesus Christ from the dead. And if that is possible, then I can do all things through Christ who strengthens me (Phil. 4:13). The context of that verse, by the way, is suffering.

Second, I know that my hardship is not pointless. God works all things for the good of those who love him (Rom. 8:28). It is wrong to think, as some commonly do, that God causes pain in order to bring forth something better. That's an incomplete, if not wicked, view. Imagine telling that to a father who has lost his child. The proper view is that, in a world of freedom where God allows the consequences of our freedom to be felt, he can take the worst things imaginable and use them for our good. All pain is redeemable in Christ.

Many times throughout the last several years, I have said that I hate what I am experiencing, but I like who I am becoming. God's grace and kindness were ever present in the midst of my hardship. I saw him working in my wife and me. And I can hate the hardship, wish it to be gone, work to be done with it, and thank God for the goodness he is producing in the midst of it all at the same time. This knowledge produces a kind of joy in trials because I know what trials produce.

Third, I know that my hardship does not rob me of a meaningful life. My ability to love God and love others is not eliminated by disability, failure, sickness, loneliness, anxiety, depression, or any other kind of hardship. A life of hardship that glorifies God in creative and sacrificial love has no rival. It is not subordinate to a life of health, success, and prosperity.

Fourth, I know that my hardship is not punishment. There are examples in the Bible where God judged someone for their sin by taking their life, inflicting them with something like blindness, or punishing them in some other way. These examples are rare and were done for a very specific purpose, which was explained by some form of special revelation.[5] Outside of God divinely revealing to you that he is punishing you for sin through your hardship, you don't need to think that.

In fact, there is a clear example in the New Testament where Jesus corrected this sort of thinking. In John 9, Jesus and his disciples came upon a blind man. The disciples asked Jesus if his blindness was the result of his or his parents' sin. Jesus said it was neither, but that the works of God might be displayed in him (John 9:1–3).

Anyone who reads the Gospels will see quickly how much Jesus cared for the afflicted. He went out of his way to welcome the sick. He even stopped on his way to Jerusalem, knowing his death soon awaited him there, and healed a blind man everyone else was trying to silence (Mark 10:46–52). Our default position ought to be to think that the Lord has great compassion for those suffering, not that he is punishing them.

Many of you need to hear and embrace this. Some of you have been carrying burdens you need not carry for far too long. You did not cause your child's disability by your sin. Your lack of faith is not why your mom died from cancer. Your miscarriage was not payback for your sexual immorality in college. Ignore all the remarks of the self-righteous who made you think such a thing, and may God have mercy on them for the pain they have inflicted upon you.

There is no condemnation for those in Jesus Christ (Rom. 8:1). Now, it is likely true that your sin has created some of your pain. For example, someone who has cheated on her husband, left her family, and abandoned her kids knows the source of her own and her family's pain. But God is not punishing you. Turn to him. Repent of your sins. Receive the gift of the Holy Spirit, and may God comfort you as he redeems the pain you brought upon yourself.

## Hating the Hardship While Rejoicing in the Midst of It

You do not have to be glad for trials, but you can be filled with joy because of what they produce. There are some lessons that can only be learned through pain, and I imagine that is one reason why God allows it. I have five kids, and I have let them experience pain. It's not possible for them to know the joy of riding a bike unless I let go. And they will fall. But some joy only comes through pain. I as a flawed father know this. God surely does.

You can relate, I'm sure. Though you would never wish for that hardship again, you also rejoice in what it taught you, how it changed you for good, and the compassion it created in you for others who suffer. You, like me, would say without hesitation that you hate what you are experiencing, but you love who you are becoming. There is joy in that—a joy that doesn't erase the pain but allows you to endure it.

You can look to "Jesus, the founder and perfecter of our faith, who for the joy that was set before him endured the cross, despising the shame, and is seated at the right hand of the throne of God" (Heb. 12:2), and take comfort in the knowledge that pain does not have the final say. Pain is not wasted if you trust in the Lord. It can bring you joy. Don't miss it.

First, when you experience hardship, turn to God's Word. Ask the Lord for his Word to illuminate any sin in your life so you can repent. It could be that your hardship is in some way a result of your sin. Again, not a punishment but a consequence. We all know the person who thinks they lost their job because God was testing them when the reality is they lost their job because they were a prideful, combative, and incompetent employee. Without the willingness to consider your sin in the midst of hardship, you're likely only to experience its pain and not receive the gift of a renewed character.

Second, when you experience hardship, turn to others. This is actually one of the greatest gifts that come in the midst of trials: true friends. I'm sure you could tell your own story, but the deep love that is given and felt when you stand alongside someone and endure their trial with them is priceless. Some of the dearest friendships that bring me the greatest joy were forged during a trial. Yet we often miss this because when we're in pain, our inclination is to withdraw. We want to be alone, and we don't want to be a burden. But be a burden. Let others help you, suffer with you, and rejoice with you as you together experience God's faithfulness. You may actually be robbing another of joy by carrying your burdens alone.

Third, when you experience hardship, turn to the Lord. God will sustain you and sanctify you through your pain, but you might not want him to. It is natural to get angry with God for letting this hardship happen. It is easy to become so embittered that you don't want to turn to him, because you don't want him to get any credit for helping you through the pain he could have prevented. I get it. But put down your fists and lower your guard. It is safe to be vulnerable with God. He will not exploit you, and he can handle your anger. Draw near to him during this time.

Strangely enough, though the enemy will try to use your pain to crush you and destroy your hope in God, the opposite can happen. That is why "we rejoice in our sufferings, knowing that suffering produces endurance, and endurance produces character, and character produces hope, and hope does not put us to shame, because God's love has been poured into our hearts through the Holy Spirit who has been given to us" (Rom. 5:3–5).

Pain does not have to crush you and make you despair. It can actually do just the opposite. It has done so for me.

## What This Means for Me and My Family

My wife and I know hardship. I could tell you several of our stories, but I'd like to end by telling you about our son Aaron and how the knowledge of what makes life meaningful has saved us.

Aaron, among several other conditions, has a rare genetic disorder called KCNB1. He is one of four people in the world to have this specific genetic mutation. There is virtually no one who knows anything about this or can help. We've been told by world-renowned geneticists to come back to them when we learn more about this disorder. It is a lonely place.

What comes with KCNB1 is a range of developmental issues and seizures that can be severely debilitating or terminal. Fortunately, Aaron does not have clinical seizures, though it is not certain that he won't in his future. And his future is uncertain.

Aaron struggles to read, and he may never do so at a useful level. He can't do math. His verbal skills are diminished, and he is generally immature for his age. But he is such a sweet boy who loves his family and friends, baseball, and Metallica. It would be such a gift for him to learn how to play the guitar. He loves strumming one, though he may lack the ability to ever learn chords. His life is one of joyful challenges.

My wife and I love Aaron, and we hate his condition. We will spend our lives seeking to cure it. We may go bankrupt doing so. But even if we never fix anything about Aaron, he is still made in God's image, he is worth more than we can imagine, and his life contains the same dignity and honor as the lives of the rest of us.

We are right to be sad. Even as I type this, I cry. Aaron may never marry, have a "real" job, go to college, play baseball on a team, or be able to experience a number of other good things. We are right to be angry that the world will diminish his value, look awkwardly at him, not give him the time of day, and do its best to ignore him. We can grieve that, hate that, fight that, and mourn that, but what we can't mourn is the dignity of our son.

It would be hard to tell you how comforting it is for my wife and me to know that though Aaron's condition may be hopeless, he is not. Aaron may spend his entire life never achieving or participating in what we commonly think contributes to a meaningful life, but his hardship doesn't make his life matter any less. His life is every bit as meaningful as yours and mine. He can know God, love God, love others, and live out his life to the end, enjoying many of the good gifts God gives us all. He bears God's image, and one day he will fully bear the presence of God with his renewed body. And until that day comes, I will be both happy and sad for my son and seek to love him the best I can.

Perhaps you think that all of this is just wishful thinking on my part. Maybe you think that I've simply found a way to cope with the pain in this life. Maybe so, but the fact that I've found something that helps me doesn't mean it's not true. And if God raised his Son Jesus Christ from the dead, then I don't think I'm foolish to believe that what he said is true about this life or the age to come. Pain will be an inevitable part of this world, but it is not a gratuitous part. I can take comfort in knowing that my pain is part of God's wonderful plan to share his goodness with us. And I will cling to that hope until it is realized or I am crushed beyond despair.

9

# Fighting for Joy
# When It's Gone

The joy that comes from knowing God and being able to live out our meaningfully valuable lives is an abiding joy. It is ever present, though there are times when we are more aware of it than others. And that is because, as we have already seen, there are things in life that suppress our joy, cover it up, or steal it from us in a sense. We must fight for the joy that is found in God and resist what is coming against us.

It was my fortieth birthday party, and I was surrounded by good friends, old and new. My wife had been trying to plan something special for me for nearly a year. This party had friends I hadn't seen in years, good food, good stories, good cigars (I love cigars—judge away), gifts, hugs, and laughter, and I didn't care one bit. I was nice. I was sociable. I laughed. I ate. And no one knew anything other than that I was having a good time. That is, except for my wife.

One day shortly after the party, I was sitting on our back patio working on something or other—a sermon, a paper, maybe this book—and my wife came out and sat next to me. And the tears came. I felt dead inside. I had never known not caring. What was this demonic presence that kept me from enjoying things I know are good? Was this going to be how life was from now on?

Apathy is the worst. It's a passionless existence. Nothing really hurts, and nothing really feels good. It is like the total suppression of joy. I imagine you've experienced something like it.

It has been said that we are in an apathy epidemic, that we are "overdosing on shrugs."[1] But apathy is not something we are powerless to fight. I think there are several things that contribute to it, and there are some practical things we can do to overcome it. Our meaningfully valuable lives do not have to be lived out in the bland land of "whatever." However, before we talk about how to fight apathy, there are two important things to know.

First, apathy is not depression, but it can be hard to tell the difference.[2] Psychological illnesses in general can be hard to discern. Anxious depression, for example, is a relatively common syndrome.[3] It has been reported that nearly fifty million adults in the Unites States suffer from mental illness.[4] Psychological disorders are very common and nothing to be ashamed about, but you probably shouldn't try to sort out on your own what you are experiencing. If you have found this book helpful so far, trust this advice: go see a counselor.

Second, whether you are experiencing apathy, anxiety, depression, or a combination, there is nothing wrong with you any more than there is with everyone else. Your psychological brokenness isn't any worse than someone else's physical brokenness. There is no shame in seeing a cardiologist, and there is no shame in seeing a psychologist.

Don't let your pastor, your friend, or anyone else convince you that you simply lack the faith they think they have: "If you just trusted in God more, you would be happy." Maybe, but do you tell your friend with cancer, your husband who lost his job, or your grandmother with cataracts that if they just had more faith, all their problems would go away?

Trusting in God is an essential part of life. If you are afflicted with anything, ask the Lord to take it away. He may—he surely can—or he may supply you with what you need to fight it and become more like Jesus because you did.

So with that being said, let us consider some of the things that contribute to apathy and what we might do about it so that our joy can resurface. Let's see how exhaustion, guilt, ingratitude, and worry steal our joy.

## Exhaustion

I think exhaustion was the biggest reason for my apathy. I work hard. My wife works hard. We have five kids. Enough said.

Actually, it's not hard work and five kids that cause me exhaustion. It's not resting. It's not honoring the Sabbath. It's not leaving outcomes in the Lord's hands. And it's not being able to let bad things go, knowing that I may not ever fix them.

I generally don't like talking about myself or my struggles, which is what everyone says before the "but" comes. But, like I've already said, the last several years have been hard. My wife and I have been working endlessly to figure out what is medically going on with Aaron, minister to all the different needs in our church, combat the lies in society through writing and public speaking, raise our kids, date each other, and reconcile the personal offenses that have come our way. And we don't like to lose.

We want good to triumph, people to follow Jesus, sickness to be cured, and relationships to be healed. But we can only fight so long before we give out. And it's not a physical exhaustion; it's a mental one.

There are some things that can't be fixed and can't be controlled. No matter how hard I try, often the exact opposite of what I'm working for happens anyway. The couple gets a divorce, the family leaves the church, a friend gossips about me, the student rejects God, and the sickness remains. Eventually, "Why bother?" finds a nice home in my heart.

"Why bother?" didn't stop me from working hard. It stopped me from enjoying the good things in life. I was plagued by this virus of an idea, this parasite in my mind, that slowly took over. If the divorce can't be stopped, if the friendships can't be saved, if the stupid ideas of the world can't be destroyed, what's so great about this birthday party? "Why bother?" spread from where it began and took over all the things I care about.

The reasons you work so hard might not be the same reasons I work so hard. Again, this is why seeing a counselor can help. Self-awareness can be difficult. Often we do not know why we do what we do, and knowing the specific problem is often what we need to remedy our condition. Still, what we all need to do—those of us who work too hard—is to rest.

Don't give in and quit, but be still and know that he is God (Ps. 46:10). And be still for a good amount of time! Stop working long enough to forget about your work and maybe even get bored. You can do this unless you believe that you are the one in control of all things. Go take a nap. God is awake.

Take a long vacation, set aside Sunday afternoon for the rest of the month to do nothing, turn off your email and social media notifications for the weekend, and maybe, just maybe, see if you can turn off your phone for the evening. And get a hobby. That may sound silly, something to tell a child. But children don't struggle with apathy. They play.

Resting doesn't only mean taking a nap and doing nothing. There is a paradoxical sort of rest that involves doing something. It is rest, but it is not a passive rest. It's recreation, re-creating. We were made to enjoy creating. It gives us life. And though our work has an aspect of this, work also has a grind to it that golf with some friends on a nice day does not.

One of the best things I did this last year was pick up the guitar again. And I did so just because I needed a hobby. The practice, the gear, the songwriting—it's wonderfully fun, and it lets me let go of work. I didn't realize that what was missing from my life was something as simple as a time to play.

My birthday last year was marked by a profound darkness. My birthday this year will be marked by a great gift. A dear friend of mine who is moving far, far away gave me a handmade boutique guitar tube amp. It's a once-in-a-lifetime kind of gift. It's rare, it looks amazing, and it sounds unbelievable. Every time I go into my office, I'm reminded of my friend and I'm enticed to play. And I do, often now. Even just five minutes of playing "Yellow Ledbetter" by Pearl Jam is enough to forget work for a moment, to be enlivened, and to remember and enjoy the good things in this life. Ideas are like viruses, and good ones spread just like bad ones. You'd be surprised how the simple thought "This is fun" spreads to all the other things in your life.

So go find a hobby. Find something you enjoy that allows you to check out and let go of your work, your cares, and your responsibilities. Your life is too valuable to be wasted in not caring.

## Guilt

Being plagued by what you have done is a disease that will kill your emotions, distort reality, and cover up your joy. Now, there are things in your past and present that you should feel bad about. The solution, though, isn't to excuse what you did, to hate yourself, or to just stop caring. Rather, repent of your sin and your pride. Draw near to Jesus. There is nothing that can separate us from the love of God. You don't have to think you're the only one God can't forgive.

There is nothing new under the sun. What you have done has already been done, and somebody is going to do it again after you. The Lord knows this, has forgiven others of this, and will forgive you too. We are such terribly prideful people, and our pride surfaces in the strangest of places. Why do we think that our sin is somehow more powerful than the love of God? Do we really think our offenses can overpower God or that his power to love and forgive is somehow beaten by what we do, however bad it is? What hubris.

God forgave King David, who committed adultery and then had the husband of the woman he slept with killed (2 Samuel 11). God forgave the apostle Paul, who, before his conversion, went from house to house dragging off Christians, putting them in prison, and presiding over some of their executions (Acts 8:1–3). God has forgiven a countless number of people, even some who were responsible for having Jesus crucified (Luke 23:34). And let's not kid ourselves. We are all culpable in that. Our sin is the very reason Jesus came to die and willingly surrender to the shame and the pain of the cross.

Why is your sin so different from everyone else's? It is time to let it go. Repent of your sin, and live in the times of refreshing that come from God's presence and his forgiveness. God will forgive you. He will even comfort you in the midst of your grief over what you have done. What kind of love is this!

Choose to live in what is real. Your life's meaning is not defined by your worst mistake. God forgives sinners. Those who ask for mercy receive it from God. He is quite generous. Do not live in your guilt. Live in the freedom and joy of knowing you are forgiven.

One thing that helps with guilt is to talk to someone about it. But not just anyone. Talk to your pastor or a trusted friend who is maybe a bit older than you and can do more for you than say, "Man, that sucks." Talking about your guilt allows you to hear the validation of another who knows that God forgives. This wise friend may also be able to tell you what to do next.

Guilt needs your atoning—first with the Lord, whom you have wronged by your rebellion, and then with the one you have wronged on earth. Now, don't misunderstand. You do not earn your forgiveness; it is given because of God's grace. However, if you are truly sorry for what you have done, you will be like Zacchaeus, a tax collector who, in his repentance, sought to make things right with those he had wronged (Luke 19:1–10). Turning from wickedness, finding forgiveness, and seeking to make right what you have wronged, if possible, can turn your guilt to joy.

Do not live in guilt. It will numb you. Rather, step into the warm light of confession, repentance, and God's mercy.

## Ingratitude

I remember when I was a kid and Nintendo first came out. I desperately wanted one. My parents weren't prone to getting us something just because we wanted it, but my grandfather might have been. He was in town, and my brother, Brian, and I started working him hard. My parents caught on, but rather than steal the joy of my grandfather buying his grandchildren a gift, they told Brian and me to go to the basement and learn contentment with our Atari. We knew what that meant. Grandpa was buying us a Nintendo.

And it was great. Of course, it wasn't long after that we were begging for something else.

Why is what we have never enough? We all are seemingly more concerned with what we don't have than being grateful for what we do have. This is the world my five kids live in. They can be so ungrateful. It doesn't matter what they have; it's never enough. But do we ever grow out of that?

I'm not sure I have a ton of great advice here. I bought three new guitars this past year. There is something intoxicating about pursuing something new. The excitement of new things can be addictive. There is, of course, nothing wrong in principle with getting something new. Part of the life-giving nature of many hobbies is the collection: the hunt, the deal, the rarity. Before long, though, we are slaves to the hunt. We obsess over new things, get new things, but never really enjoy anything. We are such fools.

We must learn how to be grateful. We must learn to say thank you. We must slow down and love what we have rather than covet the possessions of others. And though I said I may not have a ton of advice here, I do know one thing that helps: giving.

Those who are generous are joyful and content. You know this is true, don't you? You have tasted it. Some of the greatest times of contentment have come while you were serving someone else. Why is this? It's so counterintuitive. You find life and joy by giving yourself away. Maybe it is a reward that is hardwired into fulfilling your purpose to love others.

I do think one reason serving others is fulfilling is because we learn to be happy in someone other than ourselves. We become outward-focused rather than self-obsessed. We become like a happy hobbit at the end of The Lord of the Rings and not a Gollum.[5] So although I don't fully know why this works, my advice to you is to go serve someone if you are struggling with a lack of gratitude and contentment. Give some money away. Share your toys. Or you can spend your life never really enjoying anything as you hoard and covet what's next.

I do know one other thing. You are not more deserving of good things than anyone else. Often we are ungrateful because we think we deserve what we get. *Why should I say thank you when you should have gotten me that or done this for me? Don't you know who I am?* Yes, we do know. You are made in God's image, as is everyone else. You don't deserve special treatment. (Some really need to dwell on this point.) You are not worth more than anyone else. Therefore, serve others, give generously, and leave your ungrateful sense of entitlement behind.

Entitlement is often connected to insecurity. You need possessions, and you need people to validate you. But if you are secure in your identity, you know that the new car, the new house, the new outfit, the new whatever, cannot make you worth more than you are. Neither can they satisfy you in the way you hope. You were not meant to be satisfied only with created things. You were meant to be satisfied in the Lord and then experience the goodness of his creation in a pure, unadulterated way.

If you are battling discontentment, consider that you are making idols of good things. Turn to the Lord. Spend time in his Word and in prayer. And stop seeking a kind of fulfillment in stuff that can't be had.

## Worry

Worry will wear you out and bring in apathy if it doesn't kill you first. The what-ifs in life will end us, won't they? And there are reasons for them. Jesus himself said that in this life we will have trouble. Even in the great passage on not worrying, he tells us to let the troubles of tomorrow worry about themselves because today has enough trouble of its own (Matt. 6:25–34). This is one reason why I love the teaching of Jesus, by the way. He's honest.

Worry can be debilitating. It can lead to fear that immobilizes us or causes us to act irrationally. Or it might cause us to stop caring altogether. Something can't stress you out if you have given up caring. Anxiety disorders are increasing, and this world is a troubling place. The year 2020 has had more than enough trouble, but it won't be all that unique. Trouble will always be, and if we don't learn how to deal with worry, we will never be able to enjoy the gift of a meaningful life.

I'm sure the things you are concerned about are reasonable. Most of the things I worry about are worthy of worry. I should be concerned with the well-being of my family, my reputation, paying the bills, injustice, and much more. Not caring what comes of these things would be irresponsible.

So how do we attend reasonably to the troubles of the day before we stop caring about them? There are a few keys.

First, put your worry in the context of what makes your life meaningful. Is life merely about what you will eat and drink, your career, and your bank account? No, of course not. But you may be choosing to believe it is.

Think about it like this. If the thing you are worrying about should come to pass, what would it suggest for the meaning of your life? Do you now possess a life of insignificance? Maybe culturally you have lost value. Maybe your peers look down on you and consider themselves to be worth more than you. Maybe life is now harder. But your life is about something so much greater than what you are worrying about.

Much of our worry pertains to our social status. The reason we are worried about these things is because we often attach our worth to what others think about us. Let that go. A good reputation is something to be sought, for sure. But you don't earn a good reputation by worrying about what others think of you. You earn it by concerning yourself with the kingdom of God and his righteousness. Do what is right, and trust the Lord to add to your life the things that he knows you need (Matt. 6:33).

Second, put your worry in the context of time. Does tomorrow exist yet? Let me rephrase before we get into a philosophical discussion of theories of time.[6] Do you know for certain what tomorrow will bring? No, of course you don't. Any number of things can happen to change what tomorrow will bring. What good is it to worry about what may be? If you are going to worry, worry about what is in front of you.

Jesus rhetorically asks if we can add an hour to our life by worrying (Matt. 6:27). I think this is a brilliant question. No, we can't. Tomorrow's trouble is going to come whether we worry or not. All our worry does is add torment to today for what may come tomorrow. This is insane. Moreover, not only does worry not add time, it wastes time. Rather than spend time worrying about what tomorrow's trouble might be, attend to today's trouble. The present is never as frightening as the future.

Third, deal with today's trouble in the context of God's knowledge and provision. God loves you and knows what you need. If he cares for things in his creation that he loves less than you, will he not also care for you (Matt. 6:26–31)? In times of worry you may take the situation into your own hands and do terrible things because of your anxiety. Rather, trust the Lord to provide. In the midst of today's trouble, do what is right, and leave the outcomes to God. You cannot control them anyway.

Fourth, put your worry in the context of knowing God. Without having a proper relationship with God, you should worry. Even if you should gain the whole world, what will it profit you when trouble takes you? But if you have repented of your sins and placed your faith in Jesus Christ, death, the greatest worry of all, is not the end but a door to life everlasting.

Having right standing with God frees us from worry, because even if the troubles of this world overtake us, what have we lost? Knowing that in Christ we have access to the Father, are awaiting an inheritance, and have been given his Holy Spirit allows us to live freely and without fear. Come what may, nothing can take from us the thing of greatest value: knowing Jesus Christ. Even if our lives are taken from us, we have only gained, as we will be with our Savior.

This knowledge should allow us to love others rather than worry about ourselves. It should propel a life of fearless service. There is nothing greater than knowing Jesus Christ our Lord. No one can take anything away from us that will diminish our greatest source of joy.

So do not let your work, your guilt, your possessions, or your worry overtake you such that your joy is lost. Apathy does not have to be your reality. Remember who you are. You are made in God's image. You have the capacity to know him. You have been given a noble calling. You have been given God's Word and his Spirit. You have all that you need to overcome the trials in this life and experience the joy you were made for.

# 10

# The Joy in What's Really Real

We come to the end. And yet, I suspect for some of you there are still the nagging questions. Does any of this really matter? Does this knowledge make any difference? Does it really change anything? You may think, *I know what makes me valuable. I understand my purpose and the freedom I have to live out that purpose. I have a better sense of who I am, what I should do, how I should treat others, and how to endure hardship, but I still feel awful. I can't get no—bah dah dah—satisfaction.*

Mick Jagger was right, wasn't he? Though we try and we try and we try, satisfaction evades us. It is like those dreams we have where we know we can fly but just can't quite seem to get off the ground. Is God a trickster? Just as we enter a time of happiness, tragedy strikes. We fall in love and cancer finds

163

us. We get promoted and our coworkers resent us. We make a new friend and an old one betrays us. It seems all of life is simply goodness being chased away by badness. It seems that nothing we do really matters. Like the writer of Ecclesiastes said, *Hevel, hevel,* all of life is like chasing after smoke.[1]

## Nothing Matters

At first glance, Ecclesiastes seems like a strange book to be in the Bible. For twelve chapters it says over and over that nothing we do really matters. As soon as you find happiness, success, wisdom, or wealth, something happens and it all goes away. Pursuing a meaningful life is as vain and futile as trying to chase the wind.

What does all of your work bring you even in the midst of resting well? The knowledge that whatever you accomplish, you are going to eventually have to leave to someone else. Who knows if this person will be wise or foolish and squander everything you have earned? And should you even accomplish something great, who will care in the future? Time eventually erases everything you do. No one will know who you are or care what you accomplished after you are gone. This is *hevel.*

What do possessions bring you even if you don't covet what you don't have? You can spend your entire life acquiring wealth and then be too old or sick to enjoy it. You will eventually have to pass it on to someone who didn't work for it. Who knows if they will appreciate it or squander it all while not caring one bit about what you have done for them? This is also *hevel.*

What does pleasure bring you? You can indulge yourself in all kinds of pleasure; the morning always comes. Hunger returns. The heart still aches. The ear cannot hear enough and the eye can never see enough. No matter what you enjoy, you are left wanting. This is also *hevel*.

What about wisdom? What does it give you? Not much. We've all seen the fool prosper and the wise suffer. The wise and the fool both get sick, lose jobs, and suffer many of the same kinds of torments. What does your wisdom really profit you? This also is *hevel*.

Lastly, what about righteousness? What if you've dealt with guilt appropriately and tried your best to do what is right? What does your goodness give you? Not much. We've all seen the good die young, even at the hands of the wicked. The righteous suffer and the wicked prosper because of their wickedness. This too is *hevel*.

And so it is that all of our work, money, pleasure, wisdom, and goodness seem to have a vain quality to them. None of them can produce what we hope they will. Life seems to have its way with us regardless of what we do. So why bother? Nothing matters. And for twelve chapters, Ecclesiastes tells us this over and over again. But the point of Ecclesiastes isn't that nothing matters. It's actually the opposite.

## Everything Matters

> The end of the matter; all has been heard. Fear God and keep his commandments, for this is the whole duty of man. For God will bring every deed into judgment, with every secret thing, whether good or evil. (Eccles. 12:13–14)

Everything we ever do is seen by God and will be judged by him. Every word we've spoken, every thought we've had, everything we've ever done, even the things in secret will be judged by God. No, it's not that nothing matters. In a surprise twist, Ecclesiastes teaches us that everything matters. And it matters in a way infinitely more important than we realized.

So how does this bring us hope or satisfaction in life? It seems to make things worse yet again. And without the knowledge that God will pardon us of our sins on the basis of Jesus's death on the cross, it would be the worst news ever. But because God will forgive us, we need not live in fear of the consequences of our sins. We can live with the hope that, though our actions may not produce what we hope they will, God sees everything we do. That is infinitely more significant.

Don't miss that God will judge your good deeds as well as your bad ones. Now, you can take that to mean that God will show you how your good work really wasn't that good after all. That may be part of it, but God is not like your boss, who may never be proud of you or appreciate your work. God loves a cheerful giver, and whenever you serve the least of these you are serving him. Because of his grace and your faith, you can look forward to one day hearing the Lord say, "Well done, good and faithful servant."

So, though your work may not produce what you hope it will, God sees it and knows your heart. He knows that your boss is prospering through wickedness and that you are suffering in righteousness. He knows that you speak graciously while others gossip about you. He is a good Judge, so rest easy. And remember that those who gossip and those who scheme cannot control this life any more than you can with your gentle speech and loving service. This knowledge can lend itself to our finding some satisfaction.

We cannot control outcomes. This is the aspect of life that is meaningless. No matter how hard we work toward good ends, outcomes are entirely outside of our control. There are a myriad of things that can wreck our good intentions. We have power, no doubt. Our planning, our work ethic, our wisdom, and our cooperation can accomplish much. They cannot control the future, though.

If you try to control what you cannot control, you are going to be miserable. This is part of the purpose of Ecclesiastes. Let go of what you cannot control. This is the nature of life. Trust in God and recognize what you have no power over. Learn to enjoy your life as you actually experience it, not as you want it to be.

## Recognize Where Joy Is

Many of us live for future joy and neglect present happiness, subsequently missing both. So much of life is working for something, anticipating something, and as our eyes are always seemingly fixed on the future, we miss the only chance we have to enjoy something: the present. Ecclesiastes reminds us to enjoy the simple gifts God gives us: a good meal with a good woman, a laugh with a friend, and the nobility of giving a poor man something to eat. These are the things that make us full, yet we miss them in the vanity of trying to control what we cannot. All we have at the moment is a chance to enjoy the work we are given, the friends we find, the family we belong to, the ocean we are in front of, the story we are listening to, the music we are creating, the stranger we are helping, and the book we are writing.

I hope this book is used by God to change the lives of millions, and I hope it does a number of things that could bring me and my family happiness. But it may not for any number of reasons. All I have at the moment is the opportunity to enjoy the privilege of writing this book. It would be a great shame to focus on the future happiness this book *might* bring while missing out on the present joy of writing it.

Not everyone gets a book deal and has a wife who will let him write a book. I could spend the entire time being stressed over what I can't control, or I can let go of this book's outcome and enjoy it right now. I can love each word as it flows from my fingers to the keyboard. Laugh at what I want to say but could never put in a book. Cry as I am moved by a realization that was previously hidden from me. I can love and enjoy this book in a way you never will. I have been given a good thing to enjoy. It would be an ironic shame for me to miss the joy of the book because of the book.

Please don't misunderstand this point and reduce it to some sort of hedonistic "live for the moment" kind of advice. It is certainly good to be wise and plan. There is even enjoyment in both. Just remember that there is a certain vanity to planning. Plan for good outcomes, work for good outcomes, anticipate the joy of future outcomes, but do not do so at the neglect of the present. Do not live your entire life in a world that doesn't yet exist and miss the one that does.

What are you missing? It's not too late. Your kids may be older, but they are still your kids. Give them a call or pick up a glove and ball and go have some fun. Your love for your spouse may be cold, but this spouse is still yours. Stoke the fire, or build it again if it's gone out (and I mean with the same person, in case there's any confusion!). Your ambition in work is great, but it would be a shame to lose all of your friends, your family, and your sanity in the process.

Do not be so proud that you miss the joy in the simple things. And don't be the fool who vainly chases meaning through work, pleasure, wisdom, and righteousness, only to miss the gifts God has given you today.

So enjoy your work, not just what it brings. Enjoy your family as they are, not as you want them to be. Enjoy the simple things in life. They matter. They have what you are looking for.

## Three Keys to Living in the Joy of Why You Matter

I generally resist, probably to my own detriment, the "three keys to success" sort of thing. It feels so trite, so gimmicky, so simplistic. Truth is, I follow three things that really help me to live in the joy of why I matter. I think these things take into account all that we have been looking at, and they distill them so we usefully live out what we have learned. They are really questions that I ask myself—evaluative tools that keep me in the right frame of mind and allow me to experience joy.

### What Makes My Life Valuable?

Memorize this question and ask it regularly. Your entire life will be a battle to remember why you matter. You are going to be tempted. You are going to be told lies. You are going to have feelings of insecurity. You are going to experience pain. In all of it, when you feel the loss of joy and the doubts about the significance of your life creeping in, ask yourself if any of those things can remove the dignity and honor that come from being made in God's image. Attack your doubts with truth.

I once heard pastor John Piper say that you need to preach to yourself more than you listen to yourself. I thought this was great advice, and I have followed it ever since I first heard it while stocking shelves in a warehouse. Your feelings and your doubts don't get the last word. You'd be surprised how something as simple as regularly challenging your feelings with truth begins to change and shape you. The battle to live in the reality of your meaningful life is a battle of the mind. But your mind can be renewed and your life transformed because of it.

### What Joy Is Set before Me?

I will forever be indebted to my friend Barbara Toth. This book would not have been written without her and my wife. Many helped, but these two get the real credit. Early on in the writing process, I told Barbara about my struggle to write this book and asked her to pray for me. Well, she did more than just pray. She read every word I wrote and helped push me across the finish line. But one thing she did really crystalized things for me.

In her prayers, she said God impressed upon her Ecclesiastes, in particular chapter 2. She told me to stop writing and go read it. And I did. It was there in that chapter that God reminded me of something I had forgotten. I simply had stopped enjoying what was in front of me. I was consumed by the brokenness in this world and my job to be part of fixing it. My eyes were on the future and the past, and I was missing what was present.

You too may be missing out. It is a discipline to be present. It's easy to live in the future or the past, in the what-ifs or the could-haves.

My dad warned me about this years ago, and for many years I followed his advice. In my early twenties I needed to make a hard decision. After prayer and advice, Dad told me to just make a decision, live in that decision, and not be saddled by the one I didn't make. He said I should enjoy the path I was on, and if I came to learn it was the wrong one, then I should get on a different path and enjoy that one.

I hope you get the point and don't conclude that that's simply a much too cavalier way to live life. Rather, it is an essential part of abiding in God and his joy. After doing all you can to live well, let go of what you can't control, trust in God, and enjoy the simple gifts right in front of you. Ask yourself this day, What thing of joy is looking you square in your glazed-over eyes? It's time to wake up and embrace the joy set before you.

### What Is Really Real?

Regularly ask yourself if what has consumed your thoughts and your emotions is real. Not possibly real, but really real. Does your boss really think that about you? Will what you fear necessarily come to pass? Can that thing bring greater satisfaction? Is your worth wrapped up in your friends, your accomplishments, your social status, or your experiences? You'd be surprised how much time you live in a world that doesn't and may never exist, to the detriment of the one that does.

The quest for a meaningful life is the pursuit of living in reality. We spend so much time worrying about tomorrow, placing our significance in things that can't compare to being made in God's image, and trying to find fulfillment outside of the design of the One who made all things. We spend so much time trying to control outcomes and living in a reality that doesn't even exist. No wonder we are miserable. Rather, let us all fight to know what is true, believe what is true, and live in what is true. Truth sets us free.

What is real is that we are made in God's image, we are loved by him, we are given dominion over this earth, we are free to create and love, and there are a myriad of ways to live out our meaningful lives. What is real is that nothing can ever separate us from the love of God, and nothing we will ever do will add to or take away from our value.

Our struggle is to keep our house built on this rock. We must fight to live in what is really real.

Let me implore you to come to Jesus, the way, the truth, and the life, and to keep coming back to him. What you are looking for is in him. He will lead you in the way you are to go, teach you what is true about this life, and fill you with true life. In him is a joy like nothing else. In him you can find peace. In him you can rest. In him the quest for a meaningful life ends, and what begins is eternal, joy-filled life.

# Notes

## Introduction

1. Steven Pinker, *Enlightenment Now: The Case for Reason, Science, Humanism, and Progress* (New York: Viking, 2018), xvii.

2. US Bureau of Labor Statistics, "Civilian Unemployment Rate," accessed August 28, 2020, https://www.bls.gov/charts/employment-situation/civilian-unemployment-rate.htm.

3. John Gramlich, "5 Facts about Crime in the U.S.," Pew Research Center, October 17, 2019, https://www.pewresearch.org/fact-tank/2019/10/17/facts-about-crime-in-the-u-s/.

4. Robert Nakatani, "Top 10 LGBT Rights Developments of the Decade," American Civil Liberties Union, September 3, 2019, https://www.aclu.org/blog/lgbt-rights/top-10-lgbt-rights-developments-decade.

5. There are many who are seeking to redefine what racism means. They claim racism is not primarily about prejudicial beliefs and actions but more about a far-reaching structure of power imbalance. See Robin DiAngelo, *White Fragility: Why It's So Hard for White People to Talk about Racism* (Boston: Beacon Press, 2018).

I reject the new definition of *racism* and use the term in this book to describe hatred or discriminatory behavior based on race. For a good treatment of the movement to redefine racism, see the writings of Dr. Neil Shenvi. His response to DiAngelo is a good place to start. See Neil Shenvi, "The Worldview of White Fragility—A Review of Robin DiAngelo's *White Fragility*," *Neil Shenvi—Apologetics*, April 2, 2019, https://shenviapologetics.com/the-worldview-of-white-fragility/.

6. Drew DeSilver, "Despite Global Concerns about Democracy, More Than Half of Countries Are Democratic," Pew Research Center, May 14, 2019, https://www.pewresearch.org/fact-tank/2019/05/14/more-than -half-of-countries-are-democratic/.

7. "Forced Labour, Modern Slavery and Human Trafficking," International Labor Organization, accessed August 20, 2020, https://www.ilo .org/global/topics/forced-labour/lang--en/index.htm.

8. Max Roser and Esteban Ortiz-Ospina, "Global Extreme Poverty," Our World in Data, May 25, 2019, https://ourworldindata.org/extreme -poverty. For a detailed examination of how capitalism is responsible for taking the world out of extreme poverty, see Jay Richards, *Money, Greed, and God*, 10th anniv. ed. (San Francisco: HarperOne, 2019).

9. Juliana Menasce Horowitz, Ruth Igielnik, and Rakesh Kochhar, "Trends in U.S. Income and Wealth Inequality," Pew Research Center, May 27, 2020, https://www.pewsocialtrends.org/2020/01/09/trends-in -income-and-wealth-inequality/.

10. This is what the pro-life movement has been trying to tell the "You're not pro-life unless you're whole life" crowd for years. See Scott Klusendorf and John Stonestreet, "Pro-Life and Whole-Life," BreakPoint, January 23, 2020, https://www.breakpoint.org/scott-klusendorf-pro-life -and-whole-life/.

11. Aristotle argued that "the relation of male to female is that of natural superior to natural inferior, and that of ruler to ruled." See Aristotle, *Politics* (Indianapolis: Hackett) Kindle loc. 1695. Likewise, Plato wrote in the *Republic*, Book 5, "Do you know of anything practiced by human beings in which the male sex isn't superior to the female in all these ways?... It's true that one sex is much superior to the other in pretty well everything, although many women are better than many men in many things. But on the whole it is as you say." See Plato, *Republic*, book 5 (Indianapolis: Hackett), Kindle loc. 3.

12. Aquinas, *Summa Theologiae*, part 1, Q 93, art 8.

13. Miriam H. Markfield, "A More Perfect Union: Eugenics in America," *NAELA Journal* 15 (2019): 17–37.

14. Interestingly, many pro-choice advocates say that abortion ends the life of an innocent human being but needs to remain legal in order for women's rights to continue and equality to carry on. See Antonia Senior, "Yes, Abortion Is Killing. But It's the Lesser Evil," *Times*, July 27, 2010, https://www.thetimes.co.uk/article/yes-abortion-is-killing-but -its-the-lesser-evil-f7v2k2ngvf8.

15. This is a reference to Mark 9:24. The context is obviously different. The belief in question is not equality but the power of Jesus. Still, this passage is remarkably insightful and hopeful for us all. It shows us that

the opposite of belief isn't doubt. Simply put, there is room for doubt in those who believe.

16. According to the Brookings Institute, 51 percent of college students agree that you should shout down a controversial speaker, and 20 percent think it is okay to use violence to do so. See John Villasenor, "Views among College Students Regarding the First Amendment: Results from a New Survey," Brookings, September 20, 2017, https://www.brookings .edu/blog/fixgov/2017/09/18/views-among-college-students-regarding -the-first-amendment-results-from-a-new-survey/.

17. J. P. Moreland describes the rise in psychological disorders and his own struggle to overcome severe anxiety. His book *Finding Quiet: My Story of Overcoming Anxiety and the Practices That Brought Peace* (Grand Rapids: Zondervan, 2019) is an excellent resource to grow in knowledge about the prevalence of anxiety and depression in modern life as well as how to overcome them.

18. Oren Miron, Kun-Hsing Yu, Rachel Wilf-Miron, and Isaac S. Kohane, "Suicide Rates among Adolescents and Young Adults in the United States, 2000–2017," *JAMA* 321, no. 23 (2019): doi:10.1001/jama .2019.5054.

19. Dilip V. Jeste, Ellen Lee, and Stephanie Cacioppo, "Battling the Modern Behavioral Epidemic of Loneliness: Suggestions for Research and Interventions," *JAMA Psychiatry* 77, no. 6 (2020): doi:10.1001/jama psychiatry.2020.0027.

## Chapter 1 What Makes Our Lives Meaningful?

1. More research needs to be done to get an accurate count of aborted fetuses with Down syndrome. What exists is an estimate. I've not met a parent of a child with Down syndrome who wasn't pressured by the medical community to abort. However, based on the research that is available, the United States has an estimated termination rate for Down syndrome of 67 percent. In France it's 77 percent, and in Denmark, 98 percent. See Arijeta Lajka and Julian Quinones, "'What Kind of Society Do You Want to Live In?': Inside the Country Where Down Syndrome Is Disappearing," CBS News, August 14, 2017, https://www.cbsnews.com/news /down-syndrome-iceland/.

2. Part of the reason we are confused is that we live in a world where information has never before been so accessible. In your pocket is a portal to all the world's knowledge from the past until now. One would think that would mean we are the most knowledgeable people of all time. The problem, though, is that it isn't possible to absorb all the knowledge out there. But that doesn't stop our quest.

We are addicted to discovery. We are constantly looking for something new and never spending any serious time with what we find. We uncritically absorb a host of ideas, even contradictory ones, and they all just start to blend together. Over time we develop a worldview and begin to hold strong convictions. But when asked why we believe what we believe, how we came by these beliefs, and why our beliefs are true, seemingly few of us can give a straight answer.

This is why Summit Ministries and Ratio Christi are vital. They help train the next generation in critical thinking, theology, apologetics, and worldview. Their goal is to train a generation of passionate disciples ready to effectively share the gospel and argue for what is true in the marketplace of ideas. For more info visit Summit.org and RatioChristi.org.

3. You do not need to be ashamed of your suicidal thoughts. Many have them. Share them with others. Find someone you trust and who can help you. Mental illness is not unlike other kinds of illness. You need a professional to help. For some reason we feel more shame in admitting our minds are not well. Just as you would see a cardiologist for heart problems, go see someone to help you with your mental ones. There is no shame in that. And there is hope for you.

There are many factors that contribute to psychological disorders. Don't let your pastor simply say, "Pray more." Don't let your annoying cousin tell you to read their blog. Appropriately deal with what you're facing. See someone who knows how to help in a comprehensive manner: psychologically, medically, and spiritually. Again, there is hope. But it is not found in isolation and the council of idiots.

4. Richard Dawkins, *River Out of Eden* (New York: Basic Books, 1995), Kindle loc. 134 (emphasis mine).

5. Michael Specter, "The Dangerous Philosopher," *The New Yorker*, August 30, 1999, 20–22, https://www.newyorker.com/magazine/1999/09/06/the-dangerous-philosopher.

6. Peter Singer, "Killing Babies Isn't Always Wrong," *Spectator*, September 16, 1995, http://archive.spectator.co.uk/article/16th-september-1995/20/killing-babies-isnt-always-wrong.

7. William Rusher, *How to Win Arguments More Often Than Not* (Lanham, MD: University Press of America, 1985), 45.

8. Alvin Plantinga, a world-class philosopher, makes a strong case that belief in God is a properly basic belief, a belief that does not require additional reasons for support. He argues that it is reasonable to believe that if God exists, our nature has an innate capacity, the *sensus divinitatis*, to sense God's existence and to know him. See Alvin Plantinga, *Knowledge and Christian Belief* (Grand Rapids: Eerdmans, 2015).

9. Atheism isn't monolithic any more than Christianity is. Just as Christianity has many denominations, there are various divisions within atheism. So when I say "atheist" or "atheism," I use the word broadly to describe a belief system that possesses either the strong belief that God does not exist or the weak belief that simply claims one lacks belief in God. The result is the same, though—a worldview that lacks a God—as are the implications.

## Chapter 2  Can We Make Our Own Lives Meaningful?

1. If you are wondering if this story is true, it is. I know others make up stories to fill the pages or make their case. I do not. I have frequently been amazed at how bright and intellectually consistent the younger generations are. Often I find their beliefs more nuanced and logically consistent than those of their parents. This should give us all hope for the future. The younger generations want to know what is true. They are seeking what is true. Let us—those who belong to the older generations—help them. We need to up our game, grow in knowledge, hear their questions, and actually live out what we believe.

2. Ricky Gervais, as quoted in "Richard Dawkins—Sex, Death and the Meaning of Life (3/3)," YouTube video, 47:05, uploaded by lololllolo, September 29, 2013, https://www.youtube.com/watch?v=rYXDht09KXs.

3. For example, Susan Blackmore said we need to live meaningful lives because "it's just what this body does," and Daniel Dennett argued that we have evolved to care about our lives and have become "meaning makers." See "Unbelievable?: Jordan Peterson vs. Susan Blackmore: Do We Need God to Make Sense of Life?" Premier Christian Radio, June 9, 2018, https://www.premierchristianradio.com/Shows/Saturday/Unbelievable/Episodes/Unbelievable-Jordan-Peterson-vs-Susan-Blackmore-Do-we-need-God-to-make-sense-of-life; and Dan Dennett, "Dan Dennett on Creating Meaning in Life," YouTube video, 2:50, uploaded by Chris Johnson, December 1, 2012, https://www.youtube.com/watch?v=7fjkbm26loE.

4. Richard Dawkins, *The God Delusion* (New York: Houghton Mifflin Harcourt, 2008), Kindle loc. 403–4.

5. Christopher Hitchens, as quoted in "What Best Explains Reality: Theism or Atheism? Frank Turek vs. Christopher Hitchens," YouTube video, 2:06:18, uploaded by Cross Examined, May 23, 2011, https://www.youtube.com/watch?v=uDCDTaKfzXU.

6. Sam Harris, *Waking Up: A Guide to Spirituality without Religion* (New York: Simon & Schuster, 2014), 202, Kindle.

7. "Scientific" is used very liberally here. Sam Harris, for example, uses the word *science* to describe "processes of thought and observation that

govern all our efforts to stay in touch with reality." "Science" is used loosely to refer to a justified truth claim. See Sam Harris, "Clarifying the Moral Landscape," June 6, 2014, https://samharris.org/clarifying-the-land scape/; *Moral Landscape: How Science Can Determine Human Values* (New York: Free Press, 2010).

8. Dennett, "Dan Dennett on Creating Meaning in Life."

9. Utilitarianism is an ethical system that determines the rightness or wrongness of an action based upon the good or bad it produces—its utility. The various forms of utilitarianism that have emerged over the last few hundred years, from Bentham to Mill to Sidgwick to Singer, all have the same basic blueprint: maximize the pleasure, happiness, or preferences and minimize the pain and suffering for the greatest number of people possible.

10. I am meeting more and more students on college campuses who agree with this point. Interestingly enough, there is a #thanosdidnothing wrong and a #thanoswasright. Horrifyingly, though, many of the college students' judgment is based on what they have already concluded about the Holocaust. What Hitler and Germany carried out wasn't wrong in an objective sense; it was just a different view of morality. It is both re-freshing and terrifying to see this intellectual consistency. If one has ever wondered how German citizens let their government do what they did, one doesn't need to look further than the students of our own universities and their professors.

11. The Sensible Knave is a character introduced by David Hume in *An Enquiry Concerning the Principles of Morals*, who follows the general rules of justice and honesty but takes advantage of exceptions that he can make when doing so benefits him.

12. David Boonin, *A Defense of Abortion* (Cambridge: Cambridge University Press, 2002), 23–26.

13. Many don't realize that the Germans were killing their own people before they were killings Jews. They started with the disabled and moved on to cleanse the world of what they believed were other lower life-forms. This thinking was born out of the university and supported by the medi-cal field. Ideas are quite dangerous. And the ideas in our universities and medical practices do not look much different from those that inspired the Holocaust. For some of the ideas behind the Germans, see Karl Binding and Alfred Hoche, *Allowing the Destruction of Lives Unworthy: Its Measure and Form* (Greenwood, WI: Suzeteo Enterprises, 2015).

14. The idea that evolution is the guide for ethics is all throughout Hitler's *Mein Kampf*. "The stronger must dominate and not mate with the weaker, which would signify the sacrifice of its own higher nature. Only the born weakling can look upon this principle as cruel, and if he

does so it is merely because he is of a feebler nature and narrower mind; for if such a law did not direct the process of evolution then the higher development of organic life would not be conceivable at all." See Adolf Hitler, *Mein Kampf*, Project Gutenberg, September 2002, http://gutenberg .net.au/ebooks02/0200601.txt.

## Chapter 3  God and a Meaningful Life

1. Some think that these words each describe something different about being made in God's image. But the fact that Genesis 5:1 translates *tslem* as "likeness" shows that these words are different ways of describing the same general concept. See Ludwig Koehler et al., *The Hebrew and Aramaic Lexicon of the Old Testament* (Leiden, Netherlands: E. J. Brill, 1994–2000), 226, 1028.

2. There are three primary views regarding the image of God: the structuralist, the functionalist, and the relationalist view. Each view has its merits, though we must be careful how we attend to the Bible's ambiguity on this topic. What is clear from Scripture on this concept is powerful enough, and going further than Scripture can lead to unintended consequences.

If the image of God is equal to certain characteristics that enable us to carry out a function and enter into relationships, then it can be argued that those without said characteristics or those unable to perform the role or interact relationally due to age or disability (i.e., the unborn or those with mental disabilities) do not share the image of God as fully as another. These concepts of being made in God's image can lead to the same problems as the secular concepts of personhood. It may be best to allow the concept of *imago Dei* the same kind of ambiguity that Scripture does and allow it to serve as a placeholder to show our special connection with God and our intended reflection of him. For a detailed treatment of this subject, see John F. Kilner, *Design and Dignity: Humanity in the Image of God* (Grand Rapids: Eerdmans, 2015), 41.

3. I had to google what calculus is used for in real life. I'm not sure why this example came to mind, as I didn't know what people did with calculus. Turns out, some pretty cool stuff.

## Chapter 4  Creative Love and Our Chance for Joy

1. Several friends have asked me to share more about this. But some things are just for family, unless the price is right. So . . .

2. There is an old German word that describes this feeling. It is *Sehnsucht*: the longing for the infinite. Music and sports become like a religion for many because of their ability to bring some kind of consummation

for this longing. Not fully, of course, as we always want more. But I think what allows sports and music to tap into this longing rests in the marriage of purpose and creativity.

3. Some question if we are truly free. If God knows all outcomes, aren't all our choices predetermined? Am I ever really creative, or am I just an ensouled biochemical machine following God's programming rather than evolution's? Good questions, but God's omniscience does not negate human freedom. Simply knowing that something will happen does not necessarily have a causal relationship with the event. How God comes to know future events is a different question from if God causes all future events to happen. It is possible that God knows the outcomes of all future events because he causes everything to happen, but it does not necessarily follow that because God knows all future events, he causes them to happen. It is entirely possible that God knows certainly what I will freely choose, but his certain knowledge does not erase my freedom.

4. This is Satan's essential argument in Genesis 3. The lie he told Eve has existed all through history. The most notable example may be found in the writings of Karl Marx: "Religion is the sigh of the oppressed creature, the heart of a heartless world, and the soul of soulless conditions. It is the opium of the people. The abolition of religion as the illusory happiness of the people is the demand for their real happiness." See Karl Marx and Joseph J. O'Malley, *Critique of Hegel's "Philosophy of Right"* (Cambridge: Cambridge University Press, 1970), 131.

## Chapter 5 The Joy in Our Identity

1. See Eric T. Olson, "Personal Identity," *Stanford Encyclopedia of Philosophy*, September 6, 2019, https://plato.stanford.edu/entries/identity -personal/#:~:text=Personal%20identity%20deals%20with%20phil osophical,material%20objects%2C%20or%20the%20like; and "APA Dictionary of Psychology," *American Psychological Association*, accessed August 31, 2020, https://dictionary.apa.org/identity.

2. If you want a not-so-simple account of identity that even includes whether transworld identity—the ability for one's identity to exist in other worlds—is possible, see Alvin Plantinga, *Essays in the Metaphysics of Modality*, ed. Matthew Davidson (Oxford: Oxford University Press, 2003).

3. This is the basis of Sartre's existentialism—a philosophical theory about what gives our lives meaning—that we all have seemingly embraced. Sartre argued that existence precedes essence. If God does not exist, we have no design and no purpose. We are like blank slates. We must exist first in order to create the essence of who we are. Therefore, it

is our "existing," the state of self-making, that produces our essence. The significance of our lives, thus, will be found in what we make ourselves to be. There really is no other choice if God does not exist. The maxim "existence precedes essence" came from Sartre's lecture "Existentialism Is a Humanism" given at Club Maintenant in Paris on October 29, 1945.

4. Before you judge me as a misogynistic man perpetuating an oppressive patriarchal system that uses outdated gender roles, know that I tell my boys how handsome they are and my girls that they better stand up to bullies and protect the weak. You can call off the mob now.

## Chapter 6 The Joy in Our Calling

1. This is the doctrine of vocation. See Gene Edward Veith Jr., *God at Work* (Wheaton: Crossway, 2002), Kindle loc. 14.

2. Malcom Gladwell explores this topic in fun detail in his bestselling book *Outliers*. If you've not read it, you should. See Malcolm Gladwell, *Outliers: The Story of Success* (New York: Back Bay Books, 2011).

## Chapter 7 The Joy in Loving Our Enemies

1. Tom Holland, *Dominion: The Making of the Western Mind* (New York: Little, Brown, 2019), xi.

2. Friedrich Nietzsche, *The Gay Science* (New York: Vintage Books, 1974), 191–92.

3. Friedrich Nietzsche, *Twilight of the Idols* (Oxford: Oxford University Press, 2009), 45.

4. "Unbelievable?: Jordan Peterson vs. Susan Blackmore: Do We Need God to Make Sense of Life?" Premier Christian Radio, June 9, 2018, https://www.premierchristianradio.com/Shows/Saturday/Unbelievable/Episodes/Unbelievable-Jordan-Peterson-vs-Susan-Blackmore-Do-we-need-God-to-make-sense-of-life.

5. George Orwell, "Notes on the Way," Orwell.ru, December 12, 2019, http://orwell.ru/library/articles/notes/english/e_notew.

6. The parable of the good Samaritan is one of Jesus's best. Do not concern yourself with who your neighbor is; rather, focus on being a good neighbor to all, even your enemies (Luke 10:25–37).

7. For a very insightful book on this topic, see Vishal Mangalwadi, *The Book That Made Your World: How the Bible Created the Soul of Western Civilization* (Nashville: Thomas Nelson, 2011).

8. There is a lot to unpack here, too much for this book and certainly too much for an endnote. Let me just offer a couple of resources to help you get started. Ratio Christi published a helpful and free ebook by Dr. Neil Shenvi and Dr. Pat Sawyer, *Engaging Critical Theory & The Social Justice*

*Movement*, available at https://ratiochristi.org/engaging-critical-theory
-and-the-social-justice-movement/#download. The authors have also
distilled their content for a helpful introductory article on this topic; see
Neil Shenvi and Pat Sawyer, "The Incompatibility of Critical Theory and
Christianity" The Gospel Coalition, May 15, 2019, https://www.thegospel
coalition.org/article/incompatibility-critical-theory-christianity/.

9. The National Museum of African American History and Culture
produced a chart of "whiteness" that included the nuclear family as one
characteristic. They have since taken it down as a result of public backlash.
See "Whiteness," National Museum of African American History and Culture, July 20, 2020, https://nmaahc.si.edu/learn/talking-about-race/topics
/whiteness. If you would still like to check out the poster, see Mairead
McArdle, "African American History Museum Publishes Graphic Linking
'Rational Linear Thinking,' 'Nuclear Family' to White Culture," *National
Review*, July 15, 2020, https://www.nationalreview.com/news/african
-american-history-museum-publishes-graphic-linking-rational-linear
-thinking-nuclear-family-to-white-culture/.

10. "What We Believe," Black Lives Matter, September 7, 2019, https://
blacklivesmatter.com/what-we-believe/.

11. "A human embryo is not something different in kind from a human
being, like a rock, or a potato, or a rhinoceros." Robert P. George and
Christopher Tollefsen, *Embryo: A Defense of Human Life* (Princeton:
Witherspoon Institute, 2011), 49.

12. This is the standard view in the science of embryology today.
Consider what Keith L. Moore and T. V. N. Persaud say in *The Developing Human*, an embryology textbook cited as one of the best textbooks
for medical students on embryology: "*Human development begins at
fertilization* when a male gamete or sperm (spermatozoon) unites with
a female gamete or oocyte (ovum) to produce a single cell—a *zygote*.
This highly specialized totipotent cell marked the beginning of each of
us as a unique individual." See Keith L. Moore and T. V. N. Persaud, *The
Developing Human: Clinically Oriented Embryology*, 7th ed. (New York:
Saunders, 2003), 16.

13. Scott Klusendorf, *The Case for Life: Equipping Christians to En-
gage the Culture* (Wheaton: Crossway, 2009), 31–32.

14. This is the famous SLED argument advanced most notably by my
dear friend and mentor Scott Klusendorf. For a concise explanation of
the SLED argument, see Scott Klusendorf, "How to Defend Your Pro-Life
Views in 5 Minutes or Less," Life Training Institute, February 19, 2019,
https://prolifetraining.com/pro-lifer/how-to-defend-your-pro-life-views
-in-5-minutes-or-less/.

15. This comes from a speech by Dr. Martin Luther King Jr. delivered at Cornell College on October 15, 1962. "Dr. Martin Luther King's Visit to Cornell College," Cornell College News Center, https://news.cornell college.edu/dr-martin-luther-kings-visit-to-cornell-college/?fbclid=IwA R3EvmkzAEQ2Li5MLHo34U2ii3rz-nfcCPu_kEBHZTnf4VZ3JAsBO6 TbLh4, emphasis mine.

## Chapter 8  The Joy in Our Hardship

1. Richard Dawkins, *River Out of Eden* (New York: Basic Books, 1996), Kindle loc. 134. Dawkins was arguing that this is precisely the world we live in, and the gratuitous cruelty and pain in this world are reasons to reject belief in God. But this asks the question of whether all pain is gratuitous. Dawkins does not reasonably argue that there could be no reason for pain. He just seems to accept that pain and God are incompatible.

2. Jeff Meyers, *Unquestioned Answers: Rethinking Ten Christian Clichés to Rediscover Biblical Truths* (Colorado Springs: David C. Cook, 2020). I think this is a brilliant title for a book that deals with a really important subject.

3. C. S. Lewis, *C. S. Lewis Signature Classics* (New York: HarperCollins, 2002), 47–48.

4. It has been said that Alvin Plantinga has definitively defeated the problem-of-evil objection to God's existence. The objection is that if God is all-good and all-powerful, he would both want to rid the world of evil and be able to do so. The idea of God allowing evil to remain is thus a contradiction. What Plantinga shows, however, is that there is a very likely reason why God would create a world in which evil was possible. And that reason was the value of free creatures. Plantinga argued that it's at least possible that free human creatures are something of tremendous value, and a world with freedom that results in evil is worth more than a world without both freedom and evil. See Alvin Plantinga, *The Nature of Necessity* (Oxford: Oxford University Press, 1978), 164–93.

5. For example, the flood, King David, Herod, and Elymas the magician.

## Chapter 9  Fighting for Joy When It's Gone

1. Jessica Hagy, "We're Overdosing on Shrugs: 11 Strategies to Survive an Apathy Epidemic," *Forbes*, March 8, 2017, https://www.forbes.com /sites/jessicahagy/2017/03/07/were-overdosing-on-shrugs-11-strategies -to-survive-an-apathy-epidemic/#66eeb32d3ede. Such a clever title for an article.

2. Morgan L. Levy et al., "Apathy Is Not Depression," *Journal of Clinical Neurosciences* 10, no. 3 (1998): 314–19, doi:10.1176/jnp.10.3.314.

3. Kwan Woo Choi, Yong-Ku Kim, and Hong Jin Jeon, "Comorbid Anxiety and Depression: Clinical and Conceptual Consideration and Transdiagnostic Treatment," *Advances in Experimental Medicine and Biology* 1191 (2020): 219–35, doi:10.1007/978-981-32-9705-0_14; James C. Ballenger, "Anxiety and Depression: Optimizing Treatments," Primary Care Companion to the *Journal of Clinical Psychiatry* 2, no. 3 (2000): 71–79, doi:10.4088/pcc.v02n0301.

4. "Mental Illness," National Institute of Mental Health, February 2019, https://www.nimh.nih.gov/health/statistics/mental-illness.shtml.

5. I'm not going to explain this reference any further. If you don't know about The Lord of the Rings, shame on you. Go read the series or watch the movies. Then write me a letter about how much better your life is. And if afterward you want to send me a thank-you gift, you already know I like music.

6. If that sort of thing interests you, or to see what this is even about, check out William Lane Craig, "God and Time," *Reasonable Faith*, December 2, 2007, https://www.reasonablefaith.org/media/reasonable-faith-podcast/god-and-time/.

### Chapter 10 The Joy in What's Really Real

1. *Hevel* (הֶבֶל) is a Hebrew word that literally means "vapor" or "breath" and is often translated in English as "vanity" or "meaningless." It is a word that is used to describe the part of life that is illusive, the part that vanishes just as you think you are going to grab it. It's like trying to grab smoke. *Hevel* describes the impermanence and the futility of certain aspects of life. See Ludwig Koehler et al., *The Hebrew and Aramaic Lexicon of the Old Testament* (Leiden, Netherlands: E. J. Brill, 1994–2000), 236.

**Michael Sherrard** (MDiv, Luther Rice College and Seminary) is senior pastor at Crosspoint Community Church and faculty member at Summit Ministries. He is the author of *Relational Apologetics* and a national speaker specializing in biblical worldview, ethics, and evangelism. He lives in Peachtree City, Georgia, with his wife, Terri Anna, and their five children.

# SUMMIT
## MINISTRIES

Summit Ministries exists to equip and support rising generations to embrace God's truth and champion a biblical worldview.

Since 1962, Summit Ministries has trained students, parents, pastors, and teachers with the goal to raise the next generation of believers as those who understand the times biblically and know what to do.

## Conferences • Curriculum • Books • Resources

Learn more at *summit.org*.

# PERSPECTIVES
*A Summit Ministries Series*

*Why You Matter* is a part of Perspectives—a series of books brought to you by Summit Ministries and Baker Books.

This series is a collection of works that will help readers experience God's truth in all aspects of life. As a result, our prayer is that readers will become champions of a biblical worldview who will pass their faith on to rising generations with grace and truth.

Perspectives brings together biblical experts who can walk alongside readers, exploring the most challenging issues of our day. This series will help you, your family, and your church to think biblically about every area of life.

Find out more at *summit.org/perspectives*.

# Looking for more?

**Chapter Videos**

**Scripture**

**Study Questions**

Go deeper in your understanding of what makes you valuable.

Navigate to *whyyoumatterbook.com* for videos and downloadable study materials. You'll find aids like discussion questions, correlating Scripture, and more.

Individually or together with a small group, your family, or your whole church, you'll learn more about your purpose, your significance, and your value—why you matter.

## WHYYOUMATTERBOOK.COM

# FAITHFULLY ENGAGE IN THE DISCUSSIONS YOU MIGHT PREFER TO AVOID

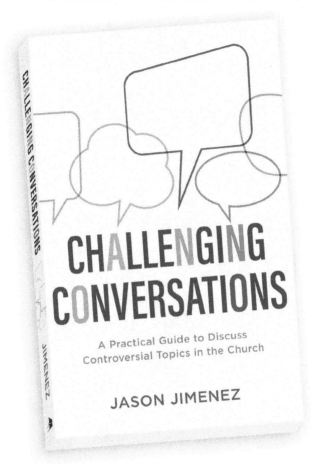

"Our world is filled with the noise of competing voices shouting about topics that make many Christians uncomfortable: sex addiction and pornography, suicide, gender confusion, divorce, politics . . . the list goes on. *Challenging Conversations* will equip you to speak clearly and confidently about God's perspective on these issues in a way that honors him and opens doors."

—**JIM DALY**, president, Focus on the Family